# johnn(y)ie

## A Memoir of Conquering the Modern-Day Goliath

by

### Johnny Dawson
### Johnnie Dixon

burning soul press

**johnn(y)ie: A Memoir of Conquering the Modern-Day Goliath**

Cover Photo Credit: Dee Dee Book Covers
Author Photo Credit: Randyll Roberts

**ISBNs:**
Paperback: 978-1-950476-94-7
Hardcover: 978-1-950476-95-4
Ebook: 978-1-950476-96-1

burning soul press

# DEDICATION

This book is dedicated to each one of you who has braved life's storms, struggled with trauma, and faced adversity head-on. Whether you are navigating life isolated amid the Appalachian Mountains or battling the opioid epidemic on Florida's coasts, this book is our offering to you. We hope it lights your path, inspires you to discover your purpose, and bolsters your faith as you overcome the Goliaths in your life.

Athletes, your journey may be arduous, fraught with momentous adversities. We commend your resolve to change the narrative of education, wealth, and life salvation in your generation. Setbacks and injuries may cross your path, tempting you to quit. However, remember, these struggles are part of your journey. Your willingness to talk about mental health struggles will break barriers and inspire countless others. We hope our stories embolden you to continue striving, irrespective of your current circumstances. Reach out to those close to you, communicate your struggles, and remember: *you are never alone.*

Marine Corps Grunts, the backbone of our defense, this book is for you. You've battled on foreign soil, in the arena, and within yourself, confronting challenges that most can't comprehend. Despite limited resources and opportunities, you've persevered, and just like in the Corps, the value you derive from life after service is of your own making. The traumas you've faced have been immense, often leading to depression, PTSD, and even suicide.

This book is dedicated to the memory of the Marines lost from 2nd Battalion 7th Marines 1st Marine Division, along with my best friend, Lance Corporal Jon Collins, and every service member lost to suicide. We also dedicate this book to athletes who struggle with depression and anxiety as they navigate their lives following their time in sports. We share our stories of vulnerability with the hope of saving a life inspired by the sacrifices others have made.

To all the selfless individuals who serve our Nation today: thank you. We honor your commitment and dedication, and through this book, we hope to offer a beacon of light, hope, and inspiration to guide your journey ahead.

To our wives, Borah and Viviana, your unwavering love and support have been vital during our battles against our mental Goliaths. Your patience and understanding have helped us weather the most challenging valleys. We cannot express our gratitude enough.

# CONTENTS

# FOREWORD

I've held hands with Johnny's darkness, sat in the pits of despair, and received wreckage I never deserved. I've struggled to find hope in our brokenness and wondered where God was. Running from my own trauma, I sat in front of a computer googling "What are the symptoms of PTSD?" I cried myself to sleep worrying about the safety of a person I loved but didn't like.

Turning to God in the darkest moments of my desperation saved not just myself or my marriage; it saved my husband. Faith, family, and deeply rooted friendships helped put the pieces of our brokenness back together.

This story began long before our paths crossed and will continue beyond our time here on Earth. It may not have started with us, but through our kids, these stories will be forever embedded in our bloodlines and carried through generations beyond ours.

My prayer for you as you look through the lenses of these two young men fighting to break generational curses, mental health, and the pressures of this world, is that you are reminded that their story, and yours, is not yet finished. Today, this month, this year is one chapter in your story. One day your story will be a chapter in someone else's survival guide. If you take that first step, your marriage, relationships, and family can be made whole.

Through hardships, trauma, joy, and love, I have learned that being Christian doesn't mean God promises an easy and perfect life. I learned this world is broken, but God is with you through the pain. God will put the right people who may be your lifeline along your path. Our greatest calling is to love Jesus and to love one another. I am proud of my husband and dear friend Johnnie for having the courage to share their stories so that you may not feel alone and know there is hope.

— Borah

My dear husband, this book is just a glimpse of the adversity you have overcome. You carry yourself with such grace while being an outstanding husband, father, son, and friend to many. God knows us better than we know ourselves, He created us, so He knows what fulfills us. Sharing your story to help others fulfills you. I am truly proud of you for the strength and vulnerability it took to share these intimate details of your life.

To the reader, as you take in the lessons within this book, you will discover a sense of my husband's strength, vulnerability, and commitment to making a positive impact. In sharing his story, Johnnie illustrates deep admiration and pride from the heart of an athlete who cares deeply for others.

This book will help any man who struggles with the pressure that life can bring. The story of *Johnn(y)ie* will shed light on your own innate ability to navigate challenges with grace and use your own experiences to overcome the many adversities we face in life.

— Viv

# INTRODUCTION

This is not a story of two best friends trying to figure out our Nation's problems. Instead, it's the narrative of two men from diverse backgrounds who battled some of life's greatest adversities in different ways. When our paths crossed, we paused and took the opportunity to get to know one another, void of premeditated biases or negative opinions about each other. Instead, through conversations, we came to value our differences, respect one another's journeys, and love each other as human beings.

After Johnny fought in combat and Johnnie battled opponents on the football field, we unraveled the darkness we faced regarding mental health. We wanted to help others facing these mountains or deep valleys. We will all learn from one another if we agree to talk about our pain, fear, personal matters, and success.

And, if we combine our efforts to bring a broader understanding of each other, we can begin to heal a divided nation.

Our book will show you how healing derives from honest, sometimes painful, conversations that lead to progress and success. We share our stories and perspectives without judgment or a lack of compassion. We plead with you to listen to our Nation's cry for humanity to triumph over all else.

This is... the story of Johnn(y)ie.

# cat(tails)

## JOHNN(Y)

**MY JOURNEY BEGAN IN** 1985 in Columbus, Ohio. At the time, my father worked at Rockwell Manufacturing on the B52 bomber as a skilled mechanic with a creative mind. When Rockwell needed more rivets for the aircraft, Dad invented and patented another way to work around it, speeding up the manufacturing process. He took his ideas to his boss, and Rockwell paid him $15,000 for the first design and $25,000 for the second, retaining ownership. Unfortunately, success came with adversity, and Dad became well-known in the area for selling his patents and the money he made from them.

Two of the guys Dad worked with were in a motorcycle gang. Initially, they asked Dad to fix their bikes, but when he got the money from his first patent, he started going to strip clubs and doing cocaine with them. Then, when he collected the money from his second patent, the same guys took Dad out, beat the crap out of him, and took all his money. I was too young to remember when Dad decided to return to Kentucky, where his side of the family lived, and my memories began.

Butcher Hollow, the once coal mining community and home of the Consolidation Coal Company, a dirt road stuck between two mountains, was where we landed in Van Lear. Mom's grandmother had family in Van Lear named Butcher. The Holler, as it was called by locals, only had one road in and out, proving to be enough for our small community. The narrow winding road into the Holler runs past an old mine shaft and the only general store, Webb's Grocery. There was a sign in the Holler that read "Welcome Home," but for us, *home* was tricky. We often moved from a rented house or trailer to apartments and even bounced around, staying with friends until my parents found another place to live. I recall my parents having to lift me up to get inside of our trailer, one resting on cinder blocks, without steps to reach the front door. Inside, a stale and pungent smell of mold filled the air. It was small, and since I didn't have a bedroom, I'd grab an old blanket and curl up on the floor most of the time.

One of the most enjoyable things about our home was that my parents constantly had music playing—Cher, The Eagles, Tom Petty, Lynyrd Skynyrd, and southern country on old 8-track tapes or the radio. The way we lived didn't bother me because I had a roof over my head and my mom worked tirelessly to ensure we weren't homeless. I didn't know anything else. Besides, most people in the Holler lived the way we did, especially once mining dissipated along with their jobs. Due to the systemic oppression of the Appalachian people, the environment was incredibly impoverished. People often bartered with each other for goods and services. Coal mining was a hard vocation and a challenging life, but the lack of jobs made life even harder, and the remnants are still there, telling the real story. Every morning, fog filled the valleys as the roosters crowed, serving as a reminder that life was a tad slower and a bit hazy.

During the day, Mom took care of me. Then, she typically worked the second shift at Food Lion in Van Lear and then the third shift at whatever second job she held. My mother was the provider because my father didn't have a job other than being an outlaw. The money Dad got from the patent was the most he'd ever made. Dad always boasted that he dropped out of school, but he's still unable to read and write. He had potential, however he lacked a vision and purpose for his life—and I got to choose to either emulate what I saw or fight to be better.

I was an only child for the first five years, and wherever Dad was, he kept me with him while Mom was working. Having that much time with Dad could have been good, but everything revolved around him getting and staying high. I was nearly six years old, sitting in the backseat while my father drove around in an old blue Oldsmobile Cutlass with his buddy, the sheriff's son. They went from one pain clinic to the next.

The only positive thing was that when my father drove with the windows down, it allowed the swirls of smoke from whatever he was exhaling to escape rather than cloud up and envelop me in the back seat. While the black cloth, partially ripped from the car roof, flapped in the wind creating a musical composition, I'd stare at the mountains, daydreaming about what could be on the other side. There had to be something else.

When we got to the place he was going, Dad would slowly turn around with glazed-over eyes and stare at me sitting quietly in the back seat. When he'd begin to say something, he had white foam built up around his lips—like he needed a glass of water. Smacking his lips, he'd say, "Johnny, stay in this here car and keep the wind'er rolled down. I'll be back after a while."

Dad didn't take me with him. Instead, he always instructed me to stay in the car while they stumbled over to a line stretching down the street with people looking just like them—disheveled, agitated, weak, and sick. I wondered what all of those people were waiting for. When they returned, they didn't waste time popping the top off a small bottle and swallowing a few pills called Oxy. After about 15 minutes or so, they seemed a lot quieter and in their own thoughts.

When I saw Dad hanging on to the steering wheel, struggling to keep the car between the lines on the road, I was afraid we were going to veer off the side of a mountain and end up at the bottom of a ravine. The relief from whatever caused their suffering was seemingly short-lived because they'd drive off to the next pain clinic, stand in another long line, and get more. I'd repeatedly watch Dad get sick off the Oxy, also known as Hillbilly Heroin. After convulsing like he was having seizures, he'd begin drooling and pass out for hours as though he'd forgotten I existed. When he finally woke up, he was still out of it. After every time he woke up, it was almost a surprise to him. In a brief period of coherence, he'd ask, "Johnny, what the hell have you been doin'?" as if I was supposed to be doing something other than wondering if he was dead.

While I never understood why he took those pills when they made him look and live the way he did, Dad didn't stop getting high. His routine was getting dangerously high. When they had another kid, Mom paid my little brother Jesse's sitter, Jackie Jean, to watch him. Though Dad was physically present, he had no emotional accountability, so I was left with that responsibility. Our parents thought it was amusing to name me John Wayne and my brother Jesse James. One was a good guy, the other an outlaw, and that's how I viewed my parents.

There weren't many boundaries in the Holler, and my father didn't have any with me. He took me everywhere, whether it was appropriate or not. Walking through the woods with him and his friend Kade Cash was an experience that most would only see in a movie. In the summer, I'd look up in childlike amazement at the towering canopy of pine trees covering the view of the sky. Everything around me was unusually lush, and the plants were more vibrant than I'd known them to be, stretching for acres upon acres, emitting a pungent, skunk-like odor. Later, I came to find out that they were vast marijuana fields.

Kade looked after us like the overseer of everything happening—or the unofficial governor of the Holler, with a wife, girlfriend, daughter, and two sons. The first time I ever watched MTV or saw a Sega Genesis was at his house, and my eyes lit up. We had a black-and-white TV, but they had more than one color television, comfortable furniture, brand-new clothes, and didn't seem to lack anything. Kade even owned a tan Chevrolet Blazer with a removable top. I'd carefully sit on the rear-facing bench seat, slowly placing my back against it since the sun had heated the vinyl seat covering, and watch the road disappear from the trailing dust cloud behind him while he drove.

We were at Kade's when Dad asked me to fetch a water pail for the chickens. I was upset that he made me help him with the chores while Kade's kids were inside playing Sonic the Hedgehog, which just came out on Sega Genesis. I smarted off and replied, "Go get it yourself!" Before I knew it, Dad and Kade took me deep into the woods in Kade's truck and dropped me off as punishment. There was a pond surrounded by tall cattails. I snapped one off its stalk and smacked it against the rock, releasing the frustration of being left. I must have smacked twenty cattails against that rock while I shouted, "I hate this holler!" I didn't know how to get home or which direction to start walking, so I stayed right where they had left me.

After an hour or so, they returned to find me with clouded eyes, a red face, and a stuffy nose, still sobbing. Waiting in that unfamiliar, heavily forested area without having any idea if they'd come back felt like an eternity. When I climbed into the back of the truck, neither of them spoke a word to me. They knew they had made their point.

I got my share of whippings with a belt, or a switch, but I was more afraid of the switch since it stung long after. High or not, Dad was quick to teach me a lesson if I stepped out of line. When Dad told me to do something, assuming he was too high to care about anything else and wouldn't know if I had, I'd ignore him and defiantly walk away. One time, I mumbled a word of profanity that I'd previously heard him use, unaware that he was right behind me. Dad grabbed me by the collar, shouting in my face, "Listen here, you little shithead! You better not use that language ever again," and then he whipped the crap out of me for cursing. After that, I was really careful about how I spoke to him.

The nature of my relationship with my father was mostly following him around and making sure he didn't die from an overdose, but whether indirectly or directly, he taught me some valuable life lessons. One of them was that I didn't need to try Oxy or any drugs to see what they did to me. Having seen what they did to my father, our lifestyle, and how they affected my parents' relationship, I was terrified. The higher the numbers went on those little pills, the sicker he got.

Every day, Dad seemed unhappy and in possession of a hopeless outlook. Wanting to be the opposite of everything he was, I focused on being happy. I tried my best not to pause long enough to feel pain and trauma, although it was there. Regardless of the adversity, I never wanted to try drugs to suppress my feelings; instead, I dug in and pushed through it. That didn't mean I never felt sad; I was terrified of losing my optimism and ending up like Dad or the broken people who stood in those long lines at the pain centers. I only had two choices: push through or lose. I wasn't going to fail.

My father was a short man, stretching to 5'7", with jet-black hair and baby-blue eyes. People said he looked like Tom Cruise or Tom Petty, and he was always working on cars. I don't think I ever saw Dad in anything other than blue jeans and a mechanic's shirt or t-shirt, with oil on his hands, nail beds, and clothing. Looking beneath the oil and dirt, tattooed on one hand was "Love," and on the other hand, across his knuckles, "Hate." And in a town lacking diversity, just above his left hand, in the middle of his forearm, he had a swastika tattoo. I asked what that tattoo meant. He looked down at his arm and then back at me with a stern, piercing stare and just said, "Power." I never knew what that meant and never asked him again.

Perhaps that was his way of reminding himself who he was since no one in the Holler feared him. Intermittently, I'd hear Dad use derogatory language towards black people, even though I didn't know exactly what it meant until I was older, especially since there was no diversity in the Holler. The things he said didn't sound right, so I didn't repeat them. On a much larger scale, I didn't mirror his behaviors either. When something doesn't seem right, it's not.

I realized that there wasn't anything about my father I should want to emulate, but I believed the way he felt came from someone. If Dad learned his behavior from somewhere, someone, or his environment, I didn't want that to happen to me. I noticed that his wrist bones were raised with huge knots on them. When I asked him why they looked that way, he said my grandmother Nelly would hit him on the wrist with a hammer, and that's just how they grew. Maybe that's where his hate or pain began. There's a beginning to everything.

My paternal grandfather was a Vietnam veteran and a moonshiner who drank himself to death, but my grandmother, Nelly, still lived in the Holler. Poor traction on the narrow, uneven, loose gravel road took us longer to get to her house. It was nothing more than a small shack with a wood-burning stove and the constant scent of burned wood. In the neck of the woods where Nelly lived, the fog was dense and mysterious, making everything feel more intense. I thought the fog knew Nelly was a horrible person, so it just stuck around.

Nelly raised chickens until they were big enough to eat. Then, she'd grab one by its head, twist its neck until its head came off, and tell me to chase it down so she could cook it. I assumed her plump, short legs couldn't move fast enough to catch a headless chicken, so she made me do it. You'd think that a chicken with no head is easy to catch, but that's not true. I was afraid to grab the chicken but equally fearful of the beating I'd suffer if I didn't. I chased that thing for a few seconds while Nelly shouted, "Dammit, Johnny! Quit messin' 'round and grab that sucker," increasing the pressure for me to tackle this headless chicken. Scared to death, I'd say, "I'm tryin', I'm tryin'!" I had the impossible task of avoiding the missing head to keep from getting blood all over my hands. I hated that chore and never understood the lesson Nelly was trying to teach me by running after that chicken. Once I got the chicken in the house, my job was to help her pluck it and clean the blood, trying to keep from inhaling its gamey smell.

Nelly was always mad about something, and she'd curse at anything, "This damn chicken," "This damn wood," and "This damn stove,"; it was always, "This damn—" *something*. Anytime I was around Nelly, I was on edge because I never knew when she'd blow a gasket and take her anger out on me.

Both Mom and Nelly often cooked chicken and dumplings but not much else. Barely enough was enough, so I appreciated whatever we had. Other than Kade, it seemed as though nearly everyone in the Holler was poor. I didn't have much to wear, and I'd never been shopping in an actual store to buy new clothing. Nelly took Jesse and me to the Salvation Army a few times, where people donated used clothes. The clothes were separated into piles on the floor, and she'd point to one of them and tell us to pick out a couple of outfits. I'd go to the jeans pile and sift through them to find a pair or two that fit. Afterward, I'd wander over to another stack and choose a couple of shirts. They were typically dirty and worn out with holes, but we needed clothing, and that's what we could afford—*nothing*. Being poor was normal. Most of the kids I attended school with looked about the same or worse, but their circumstances may have been tougher.

On a seemingly ordinary day, Mom had to work, so she dropped my one-year-old brother Jesse and me off at Nelly's. When she left, Jesse started crying and wouldn't stop. I thought he was hungry, tired, his diaper was dirty, or maybe he just missed Mom, but Nelly didn't care. She wanted him quiet. I tried my best to get Jesse to calm down by giving him toys or attempting to play with him, but he wouldn't stop, signaling Nelly to come stomping in from the kitchen.

"Dammit, Johnny, if you can't get 'im to be quiet, I'll make him quiet!" Nelly grabbed my baby brother by one of his legs and flung him across the room, raising her hand back as far as she could while storming toward him.

"No, Mamaw, no!" I yelled. When she swung at him, I screamed and kicked her in the shin with everything I had. Nelly swung around and shoved me to the floor.

"Sit your ass down, or you're next!"

I didn't care. I crawled over to Jesse, shielding his little body with mine, screaming, "Help! Help!" as though someone could save him. Even if echoes from my cry bounced off the Appalachian Mountains, no one would have come to help because this was the way of life in the Holler. Yelling for help only fueled Nelly's rage, and her wicked eyes became more vicious and *terrifying*. Nelly looked like someone or something had removed whatever good was ever in her when she lifted her leg over my body and started kicking and stomping me.

"You little shit!" she shouted, like I was nothing and no one to her.

When Mom picked us up, it took her less than thirty seconds to notice something was wrong—then she saw the bruises on my leg. Walking toward the car and feeling that we were far enough away from Nelly, I knew I had to say something.

"Mom, Nelly threw Jesse and kicked me trying to get to him," I confessed.

Mom didn't reply. She just had a crazy look in her eye when she turned around and stormed back up the dirt path to Nelly's front porch. I heard a few loud curse words and saw Mom get in Nelly's face. When Mom came back, she told me Nelly said we were misbehaving, which was far from the truth. Mom knew she was lying because she knew her kids. I didn't know everything Mom said or did that day, but I knew Nelly was no longer a part of our lives after that—I never saw her again.

---

THE COAL-MINER'S DAUGHTER, Loretta Lynn, had a property just a quarter mile from where we lived that had been turned into a tourist attraction. I'd often hop on my bike and ride it past their cabin. And even though it cost $1.00 to tour Loretta's cabin, I'd been inside her home many times just to look at the pictures of her success on the walls. I imagined that one day, like her, I'd experience life outside of here.

I spent most of my time exploring the hills behind her cabin, building tree forts or squirrel hunting with Dad when I was six and seven years old. The mossy scent of those hills hadn't dwindled; it was perfection. And the heavy white haze stretching across the mountains or thick fog evaporating with the sunrise was a sight to see. Most of my memorable experiences were spent in those mysterious hills with meandering creeks snaking through them. I surrendered to the calmness of the mountains, listened to the birds sing, and observed how everything worked in harmony. Sitting along a rock formation watching the water drip down the edge into the moss below, I often wondered, *if I kept walking through those mountains, would I end up somewhere better?*

I was always told that Loretta Lynn was a distant cousin. Loretta's mother's name was Clara Butcher Webb, but I never knew if that had something to do with the name of our holler. My grandmother's maiden name was also Butcher. I'd often hear that after my parents attended a funeral in Butcher Hollow, I was in a baby carrier laying near my dad's feet while he shot a bow and arrow behind the house. Two women walked over and started talking to dad and asked if they could shoot the bow. One of the women picked me up. The women were Loretta Lynn and Dolly Parton.

This story was our 'claim to fame' relationship with Loretta and Dolly. However, I always wondered if the story ever happened or if it was a tall tale that most old timers in the holler were good at telling. Even if the story wasn't true, it still inspired me to realize there was more to life than what I saw and experienced outside that single dirt road. Similarly, I tell my boys today that Jack Dawson from the Titanic is their great-great-grandfather and we're only here today because Rose survived. Eventually, I had to tell them the truth when one of them wanted to create a school project about their "great-great-grandfather, Leonardo DiCaprio." I suppose we didn't stay in Kentucky long enough for me to discover the truth and my grandmother had too much pride to break my heart. Maybe I mirrored my experience as a child onto my children.

Loretta's brother, Herman, had one of the nicest mobile homes in the Holler, and his property consistently had manicured landscaping and mowed grass. Located at the entrance to the old coal mine that the state closed and blocked off, it was the closest property to Loretta's cabin. The only paved part of the Holler was the parking lot out front of Herman's store, where I used to ride my bike. Herman always came out of his store and sat a Moon Pie with an ice-cold RC Cola on the ledge. I'd ride my bike over to him with a big smile. Then, he'd sit on a wooden stool and talk to me like a grandfather.

He'd say, "Enjoy your life, John Wayne. Don't go too fast, and always remember your roots, son. I know life is hard in the Holler, but it'll someday help you make it through hard times," then he'd glance around and stare at the hills. He'd take a breath of fresh air with Kade's roosters crowing in the background. Then, still reminiscing, he'd add, "Enjoy those deep woods, too. That's where you'll find peace."

I couldn't imagine anyone appreciating those woods and that pace of life more than Herman. And he was right. It was picturesque and serene in the Holler. The clock slowed a bit, allowing us time to look around and understand that life was more significant than what we believed. Trees, hills, peace, quiet—and time to figure things out. During one of our conversations, I asked Herman how to get out of the Holler. Herman laughed and told me, "Son, there's only two ways. Become famous or go to war."

"Do you think I could ever become famous?"

He grinned, "If Loretta can do it, you can do it."

# JOHNN(Y)

## FORGE • AHEAD

**CATTAILS WERE COMMON ALONG** any water's edge in the Holler. I'd often snap a cattail off the stalk and smack it against a rock to watch it explode. Watching the fibers inside catch the wind that carried the soft white seeds away was mesmerizing. I had never hit a cattail so hard in my life than when Dad and Kade left me deep in the woods. You could hear the SMACK echoing off the hillside, so loud that I hoped my father would notice. I felt the resentment towards my father starting to build. It was as if my dad was smacking my soul against a rock and the protective shell around my heart was starting to break open, the love I had for him beginning to float away in the wind.

It is amazing how we all hold a protective shell around our feelings and emotions; however, they can be easily broken—full of seeds ready to germinate new opinions, perspectives, and experiences. From a biblical perspective, cattails represent salvation and deliverance from harm, ruin, or loss. I spent many years wondering why cattails

21

were always such a vivid memory of my time in the Holler; however, as I grew in my faith, I came to believe that God wanted me to understand there was more to me than the outside, waiting for salvation.

Maybe your soul has been shaken, and you're seeking salvation, awaiting deliverance from the pain you've endured. Despite the pain, know that the opportunity to germinate new seeds of hope is ever-present. Don't allow your circumstances to supersede who you are designed by God to be. Just as a new cattail will grow the next day, tomorrow offers new hope for you.

Herman, thank you.

# fire(alarm)

## JOHNN(IE)

**BOTH MY PARENTS PLAYED** basketball in high school, Mama at Dwyer and Pops at Palm Beach Gardens, just ten minutes away from one another. Mama had the opportunity to continue playing in college, but she got pregnant with me during her senior year in 1994. Despite having basketball players for parents, I basically came out of the womb as a football player, a passion in me that was shaped by the environment I grew up in. Not long after I was born, Mama and I moved to Stonybrook Apartments in West Palm Beach, Florida.

It may have been considered the projects, but we took pride in living at Stonybrook because we were surrounded by aunties and cousins who lived there as well. We don't realize how much where we are raised will shape us; even being there for only a brief time, Stonybrook impacted who I was and my goals and dreams for the future. Especially because I discovered my love of football in the parking lot there.

The complex was small, split into two sides, and everyone knew everyone. Mama and I lived upstairs next to my grandmother's sister, Auntie Pam. My grandmother Vivian resided in the building next to us on the second floor, and Auntie Shirley, another of Grandma's sisters, stayed on the other side. My father, Johnnie Dixon, wasn't in my life that much. Although Pops lived in the same city, I only saw him around the holidays because he wanted me to see my grandmother. I was a kid, so I didn't understand grown folk's business and why I couldn't see him more. I wanted to be around my father, but figured Pops didn't have the time.

We had regular cookouts, great food, and the unity of practically everyone enjoying life together. But despite those special memories, many of the nights there were families not knowing if they were going to eat that night. Usually, one meal per day was the standard. We had an advantage having so many family members around. If our family didn't have food, we could run to someone else's house to find something.

Every single day I saw a crime, whether it was drugs, stealing, or fights breaking out, but to me, it was just the way of life. Palm Beach County was under siege from the powder cocaine and crack epidemics. Growing up that way gave me experiences to learn from, and I didn't let anything get past me, which made me tough, resilient, and a fighter.

There were laws, but they didn't help us. On the contrary, they further suppressed us. There were influential people around me who were gang bangers, drug dealers, and addicts. Although that was the norm, I stayed away from gangs and drugs, and anyone selling or using kept the gangs and drugs away from me. From what I could tell, the dealers didn't touch women and kids in the hood, and they protected the athletes. Most of the time, the older heads selling were usually some of the better athletes that had played semi-pro ball before my generation.

I think they wanted to see something different come out of the hood. They wanted to see us make it out of there. But for that to happen, I had to create a vision, and it had to be better than my environment. I didn't want my mother in that environment or working two jobs for the rest of her life. She was already making enough sacrifices, and I could see that something had to change. I had a chance to do that. My uncle and cousins didn't have the same benefit I did. Their only path was violence, drugs, or whatever the hood produced. There aren't too many options when you grow up there. You don't see too many people of color become successful.

I was the kid everyone always thought was okay and didn't need anything. That was true for the most part, but it would have been nice to have my dad around more. I've never been a needy person, but I just wanted to see him a few times a week and be noticed by him. If Pops had called regularly, I would've been satisfied, but that wasn't the case. I rarely heard from him except the occasional times when I'd show up at a family member's house for a holiday event and he would be there, too. I didn't hate or blame him for anything, but it was challenging to accept he wasn't there for me. Although I tried to conceal how much I missed Pops, sometimes his absence would make me mad at him, and when Mama saw I was hurting, it made her hate him.

# JOHNN(IE)

Grandma had me straddled on her hip if I wasn't with Mama. When I got older, I still wasn't much further away. When Mama was working, if anyone saw Grandma, they saw me, too. We were close, and she spent a lot of time with me because she didn't work. But Grandma was always paying her bills, liked her Miller High Life, and had her Newports. No matter what she was struggling through, she would talk her talk and walk her walk. Grandma was small and fiery like dynamite. I'd watch her move from zero to one hundred like it was nothing! If she didn't like someone, they knew. She played no games. We didn't have many conversations about life, but I learned from her by observing.

My mother and grandmother were strict, but Grandma let me get away with a few things when I was younger. Over time, Grandma became stricter and in moments, I thought she was the meanest woman in the world. Even then, though, I knew it came from a good place. She was a special lady, and I was influenced by her passion and fire. Even when she had bad days, you could see her heart and how she loved hard. I was a little hotheaded as a kid. Grandma definitely knew how to temper it, but there was no room for soft where we

27

lived, so she'd let me curse people out, but nothing more than that. I was called "Badass Little Johnnie," and I earned that name.

I was my mother's only child for a while, but my Auntie Tevia, another of Grandma's daughters, was only a few years older, so we were like siblings. Tevia couldn't go anywhere without me tagging along or riding on the back of her bike. It was almost a guarantee that I'd follow her wherever she went. Of course, Tevia and I had moments when we didn't get along, but what mattered was that we had each other's backs for sure, and that bond meant everything.

When I was seven, we moved to another complex, Spinnaker Landing in North Palm Beach, where my little brother, Ben, was born. I knew his father, Big Ben, before he was conceived. He lived with us at Stonybrook and then Spinnaker Landing until he and Mama separated. For the most part, Big Ben seemed okay because he always treated me right, but over time, I couldn't say that for Mama.

Mama was hardworking and no matter what, she never called off. Besides hanging with Grandma and Tevia, I was with Mama when she wasn't working. She was involved in practically everything I did, including serving as a team mom in elementary school. It was nothing to see Mama running up and down the sidelines during my football games, even when she was pregnant with my brother. She never missed a game, not one. And unless she was working, she was never far from me either. Since Pops wasn't around, Mama instilled discipline. She wanted me to do better as a young man, dream bigger, and work harder, only I was young, silly, and the class clown, so she had her work cut out.

In first grade, I went to Lincoln Elementary in Riviera Beach. One Friday, someone dared my cousin, Aunt Shirley's son, Boongie, to pull the fire alarm. But he didn't want to; he was usually the calm one, and likely wouldn't engage in something that would get him in trouble with Aunt Shirley since that would bring conflict. Living up to my nickname, I volunteered. I pulled the lever on the alarm with pure enjoyment. Seeing everyone flee the building was funny—until the principal and assistant principal pulled up in a white golf cart and snatched me up. I knew Boongie had snitched on me, and why he didn't take any of the blame—Auntie Shirley was crazy!

Surprisingly, the principal didn't do anything, and I thought I was off the hook. I should've suspected that he had another solution when he raised his eyebrows and stared at me suspiciously. He picked up the phone, called my mother, and let me go after making sure I saw his knowing smile. I wish he'd punished me and left Mama out of it because I was confident I was in trouble!

Heading home after leaving the principal, Mama drove right past me. Oh, she saw me, but she didn't stop to give me a ride home. Instead, she yelled out the window, "You're getting yo ass whipped!" and she kept driving.

She wasn't playing either. It's like she sent out an announcement and told everybody. As soon as I got home, Ben's dad asked, "Boy, what the hell you did? Your mama's gonna whip yo ass!"

And she did.

Shortly after, Mama put me in R.J. Hendley, which was a Christian school, probably because they could paddle me if I stepped out of line. But like I said, I earned the name "Badass Little Johnnie," so that meant nothing to me. I was still getting in trouble by doing silly things.

# JOHNN(IE)

One day, I got called into the principal's office, and on my way, I saw a kid coming out of the bathroom with his pants stuffed with tissue. He entered the office before me, and I heard the principal paddling the crap out of that kid. I found out why he shoved all that tissue in his pants. When I walked in, sure enough, the principal paddled me, too. It hurt, only I was used to getting whoopins, so it wasn't that bad. I'd fake cry whenever Mama got me, and she'd stop. I think it hurt her more than it did me. But since I played football, I was supposed to be tough like all athletes, so I took it.

When Grandma found out I got paddled at school, she was mad, not with me, but with Mama.

Grandma told her, "I didn't send you to no damn school to get a whoopin'! I don't know why you're sending my baby there!"

I loved my grandma. She had my back even when she didn't know I knew it.

# FIRE(ALARM)

## FORGE • AHEAD

**WHEN I PULLED THAT** *fire alarm, I knew I was about to be in the most trouble I've ever been in with Mama. When she shouted out the car window, I instantly felt a pit in my stomach and knew that I messed up. Oftentimes we don't think through the outcomes of our actions and the results on the other side of those actions. Looking back, if I knew the outcome of my action of pulling the alarm, I most likely would not have grabbed the lever and laughed as I pulled down.*

*Today, we often say things without thinking about the outcome and how it may make the other person feel. We see it repeatedly on social media. The cruelest comments you could imagine often fill your feed; the poster doesn't realize their effect on the other person. Unfortunately, every cruel comment directed at someone could be the fire alarm we're all pulling on a regular basis, creating panic, anxiety, and depression for those who may not have the* mental stability to deflect the negative undertone hurled their way.

Instead of pulling alarms, what if we looked for them? What if we recognized the dangers of these comments and offered support?

One way we can become more mindful of our actions is by using the E+R=O mindset.

### EVENT + RESPONSE = OUTCOME

With any event, there will be a reaction to that event. That reaction can be positive, or it can be negative. When you take the Event plus your Response to that event, you will come to an Outcome. For me, the event was a dare from a classmate to pull the fire alarm, my response to the event was "just do it," which in return led to a pretty bad whipping, a.k.a. the Outcome. The next time you feel a negative Response to an Event, ask yourself if it is possible to change your attitude towards that Event to create a new Outcome. You may just find this strategy to work wonders for not only your mental health, but those around you.

Grandma, thank you.

# head(lights)

## JOHNN(Y)

**I TYPICALLY WANDERED AROUND** the Holler and did my own thing, shooting groundhogs and squirrels with a 22 rifle. The races ran late as my dad would drive a '73 street model Camaro painted identically to Jeff Gordan's No. 24 Chevrolet for NASCAR. We didn't get home until two or three in the morning, even on school nights. But that didn't matter. Given there wasn't a fundamental structure, school was not a focus as a child. I didn't receive good grades, but I still passed. My mom was the main driver of me attending school; if it had been left to my dad, I probably never would have gone.

There was no structure for nutrition since I ate whatever was available. Typical meals were oatmeal cream pies, Moon Pies with RC Cola, noodles with beef chunks, boxed mac and cheese, Fruity Pebbles, and chicken and dumplings. For the most part, I had to piece meals together since Mom worked the second and third shifts, but she still used her money to bring food home. And, like Dad, I drank a lot of Dr. Pepper, though I wasn't aware that my teeth had rotted all the way across the front—attributed to a highly unhealthy diet of junk foods and sugar.

In kindergarten, we took a field trip to a dental office, and when the dentist saw my teeth, he shook his head and sighed.

The dentist looked over at my teacher and asked, "Where's this boy from?"

"That's Johnny Wayne Dawson's boy. They're down in Butcher Holler."

The dentist didn't know who I was because that would have been my first visit. Then he leaned down smiling and patted me on the head, reassuring me, "We're gonna pull your teeth. But you'll be alright." I didn't know why there was anything wrong with them. Still, his assistant put a little mask over my nose to administer laughing gas and when I was numb enough, they went to work. By the time he finished, and I could smile, he had pulled my teeth—all of them! Mom couldn't hide her shock and anger when I got home. She snatched the phone off the hook and called the school, demanding to know, "Why'd y'all pull my son's teeth? And how much is this going to cost?"

Mom seemed reassured when she realized she didn't have to pay anything. The reality was she knew the dentist would get away with pulling my teeth without consulting her. That's how the Holler operated—no real rules and no real laws, which meant no recourse.

Mom's parents, Don and Glenda, lived in Circleville, Ohio, and I believe if it wasn't for them, we wouldn't have had any type of decent life or structure. Every time they came to Kentucky, I was ecstatic because they were the most incredibly kind and compassionate people. I called her Maw-maw when I was younger, but after my cousin, Mike, made fun of my southern phrase, I started calling her Grandma like the rest of my cousins. My grandfather owned Don's Body Shop, a collision and repair shop in Circleville, and was well-known and respected in town. Grandpa was a member of the Elks

Club and Moose Lodge, and was deeply invested in the community, and more importantly, in Jesse and me. Aware of the impoverished way we lived, they weren't judgmental; they just made sure we had fun when they came to visit or when we were able to spend time with them.

Time with my grandparents was always the best, but the reality of our lives was always waiting for us in Kentucky. When we returned from Christmas break, our house was gone. A fire stole it. We stood in front of the skeleton of a charred house with a hollow roof filled with ashes. We didn't have much before the fire, but now we had nothing other than what was in our tattered suitcases.

Yet somehow, despite the adversity we faced, Dad always managed to have a temporary lifeline when he was in a bind. Since we didn't have a place to live, we stayed with Aubrey Ellsworth, another of his buddies, for a while. Because there wasn't a bed for me, I slept on the floor with his black dog, who looked identical to him. Same beard, same slow mannerisms.

When Mom and Dad pooled enough money together, we moved to a brick apartment building on another hill next to the road. Between the two apartments was a foyer on each side, and we lived in one of the small first-floor units. Mom kept the small apartment clean and continued working two jobs, but Dad hadn't changed. I'd still find him sitting in the kitchenette until he'd sway one way or the other before passing out and falling on the floor, convulsing and foaming at the mouth. I never understood what he got out of being that way because eventually, he couldn't function. He got high more frequently then, and his behavior was off. I caught him hiding an AK-47 and other guns in the ventilation shaft above the hallway. When he left the apartment, he was usually up to something with one of his buddies.

My parents occupied the bedroom on the right, and Jesse and I shared the one on the left. We had a set of bunk beds, and I taped a poster of a grizzly bear holding a Confederate flag to the wall. I didn't understand the significance of the Confederate flag and what the Confederacy represented. I viewed the flag as though it meant anyone in support was a rebel who opposed being held to an authoritative status, purely because the word "rebel" was on the poster.

I was fearless at an early age, and while some adults called me "Little Johnny", others called me a "Little Rebel." I wanted the poster because it matched my nickname. It is likely I was called "Little Rebel" because Dad was known as an actual rebel, and people in the Holler assumed that my destiny was to become my father. But my reason for having the poster didn't go beyond that—I just didn't want my life defined by where I came from because that's how people would judge me.

I was called a hillbilly, a derogatory term that means an unsophisticated country person associated with the remote regions of the Appalachians. That was the label society gave me. But I couldn't change where I came from; the Holler was my home. The hills gave me life and peace of mind. The problem was that the label stuck once people knew where I came from or heard me speak. When I left that environment, it seemed like I was different, but I wasn't.

This life had become my normal. I spent more time with Dad than with Mom at that age, harboring resentment toward her for leaving me with him. But as I got older, I started formulating different thoughts and opinions about things, which caused me to look at my father through a different lens. The people he was around were like him, and they pulled one another down. This period of time let me know I didn't want to live the way he was existing or allow the environment we lived in or his downtrodden mentality to shape me. I couldn't imagine being filled with so much anger that I'd threaten to kill my child if he crossed me.

Kids jokingly called me Evel Knievel because I was the one always building ramps and trying to do tricks on my bike. But I wasn't the only one. All of my friends were adventurous, especially my buddy Billy Silas, who was a year older than I was. If I wasn't with Dad, I would have been hanging out with Billy. We'd meet up on the cliffs, where he'd be rolling rocks off them, trying to hit passing cars. When Billy hit one of them, he took off running. I followed him. Billy took running wild and being rebellious a lot further than what I had in mind. It seemed that I was always trying to stop him from doing something reckless. But since he was older, he did what he did.

Billy was self-governed and lived in the same conditions and apartment complex as me. We explored the hills, played among the verdant hues, had fun, and inadvertently found things to get into. When we saw what appeared to be an abandoned four-wheeler, we couldn't leave it alone. Billy jumped on and started it up. When I climbed on, we took off ripping through the woods across the rugged terrain, snapping branches beneath the wheels. We flew down some steep slopes, laughing and hollering the whole time. We quickly learned that apparently, it was not abandoned. Fueled by fury, the teenagers it belonged to heard it running and came chasing after us. Billy stopped the four-wheeler and said, "Johnny, get off and go hide. I'll lead them away from here!"

Terrified, I jumped off and hid, staying in the same spot for a long time because I thought if they caught us, they'd kill us. But Billy just kept on running until they caught him. Showing no restraint, they beat him up pretty badly. That was one of our many fun adventures—until it wasn't. The way those kids beat the crap out of Billy made me never want to be a bully or intentionally cause harm.

Rebels without caution or care, Billy and I wandered the hills routinely, even venturing out late one morning in January of '94. By mid-morning, it began to snow and the winds picked up. We were doing what we always had and saw no reason to return home. A few hours later, we were deep into the forest, with the weather quickly transitioning into the heaviest snowfall we'd ever experienced. Billy and I were dressed warmly, but not prepared for the weather we would face. We layered up wearing two pairs of sweatpants and our raggedy winter coats with a few tears and white inner stuffing popping out. Typically, Mom would make me wear bread bags over my socks to keep my feet dry, but today I ran out of the house without knowing about the forecasted snowstorm.

We suspected something was wrong when the conditions turned into a complete whiteout, making it impossible to see our hands or walk in the thick, mounting dunes climbing up our calves. Swept up by wildly swirling snow squalls, it was impossible to tell one direction from another to make it home. Seemingly sentenced to be stuck in the storm that day, fear crept in. The visibility was so incredibly poor that when we crossed a creek, we couldn't tell it was one—until Billy fell in, and I dragged him out, soaked and shivering.

Numb from the cold, my focus was on getting out of that situation.

Billy started shaking pretty badly and, with a labored breath, he said, "Johnny, don't you dare leave me here. I can't feel my feet or my hands."

Although I was scared, I said, "Billy, I'm goin' to need your help, but I'll try to carry ya as far as I can."

The fear of failure had to be nothing more than an illusion. Giving up would have been more difficult than trying; besides, I had a slight advantage, so I used it. Since the landscape was somewhat instinctive, I ignored the adverse conditions and did what was necessary. I was being challenged to see what I was made of. I'd get to prove that I had what it took to survive in the hills I claimed to know and love. I picked Billy up and carried him as far as I could through the woods, stopping only long enough to catch my breath and wiggle my toes to make sure they weren't frozen.

We'd been in the woods too long, and Billy appeared to have mild hypothermia. I had to get him home or somewhere warm before darkness fell—and the temperature was dropping. Though I was afraid, I didn't tell Billy because I would've been feeding that fear. Stopping meant defeat, and we'd freeze to death. Since time was working against us, we kept moving forward, one step at a time.

After a while, I thought I saw the shape of a black pole in the distance. Though barely visible, I knew something was there. I told Billy, "Whatever that pole or thing is, we got to get to that." Billy didn't respond, but we kept going and eventually made it. The basketball hoop behind our complex was the pole I spotted—we were home! I didn't know why we were in such a severe snowstorm that day, but when we came out of it, I learned something about myself—I'd grown with every step.

After telling Mom everything that happened, she told me I couldn't go into the woods like that again. We later found out it was the historic blizzard of '94.

---

**SEVERAL MONTHS LATER,** I sat on the passenger side of our blue Cutlass with the windows down, observing the silhouette of cattails growing along the shore in the boondocks. Like a scene in a dramatic movie, the reflection of moonlight from the creek illuminated the cattails. The homes Dad parked in front of were mobile, and the cars were not. One trailer in particular was crammed with people inside and out; the smoke was just as thick as the crowd. We'd been to this trailer before because I recognized the exceptionally large wolf chained to a tree in the front. Dad always told me not to go near the wolf because it would eat me.

There was a party going on, and I could barely hear the bullfrogs croaking over the blaring sounds of Lynyrd Skynyrd's "Simple Man." Ironically, being a simple man wasn't in Dad's cards. From the look in his eyes, I knew the night would hold its own adventure. Dad wasn't in the mood for partying that night. On the drive over, we didn't talk. Not a single word. I could tell Dad was fuming and became more agitated when he got out of the car. I turned around, watched him pop the trunk, and saw him pull out a jet-black, sawed-off shotgun with a knob at the end wrapped in duct tape. Dad stuck his head back inside the window, instructing firmly, "Stay your ass in the car and don't get out! I'll be right back!"

Dad walked in front of the car, the headlights beaming. The light reflecting off the black steel of the barrel made him look like a madman storming into the trailer. Before Dad had a chance to utter two and a half words, two shots were fired, sending everyone running outside, screaming and hollering. Dad just casually walked out of the trailer and got in the car. He was still pissed but seemed satisfied, like he'd settled a score. He pressed hard on the gas and sped off, shouting, "Don't you dare tell anyone about this, or I'll shoot you, too!"

Clearly, I never did.

The man Dad shot in the foot was the mayor's son. They'd committed insurance fraud when they burned down our house, but somehow, the guy cut Dad out of the deal. Then he threw that party to celebrate getting a big check, which sent Dad over the edge, so Dad shot him.

After taking me home, Dad went back and drove his friend to the hospital. Then, holding the guy at gunpoint, he threatened, "If you tell anyone, I'll kill you!"

They claimed it was an accident, and nothing ever came of it.

# HEAD(LIGHTS)

We always had a CB radio so that Dad could listen to the police scanners and keep up with what was going on. One night a specific code came over the scanner, causing Dad to react in a panic. I didn't know what it meant, but he did. He told us to hurry and pack our things while he started grabbing some of his things and shoving them in a garbage bag. We took as much as we could fit in the car and drove to one of his friends' houses. We stayed for a month before bouncing around like nomads for a while.

Being on the run helped Mom realize that Dad's problems extended beyond drug addiction. He wasn't just an outlaw. He was a criminal. Often, the sheriff came looking for Dad, and when he heard the sirens heading in our direction, he'd take off into the mountains. The sheriff used a bull horn to yell into the mountainside, "Johnny! If you can hear me, we're planning to take your kids if you don't come off that mountain!"

Sure enough, Dad came walking down the mountain, shaking his head and yelling, "I didn't do nothin'!"

# JOHNN(Y)

The sheriff would hand Mom a $50 bill and apologize while they were hauling Dad off to jail again. After working on their police cruisers, they'd let him come home. Things were becoming uncomfortable for everyone as my dad's behaviors and habits started to place us in more danger. I could tell my mom was becoming concerned for the wellbeing of my brother and me.

After school, I walked into our apartment with my bookbag and stepped into the bedroom I shared with Jesse. We had a set of bunk beds but nothing else, and I had a clear view of the room. When I dropped my bag, the accordion closet door was pushed open like someone was hiding inside. I ran out of there and went to our neighbor's apartment, who, occasionally, was our sitter. Holly called the police and when they arrived, they found both the closet and bedroom window wide open. The police claimed that someone was most likely there to kidnap me—probably due to Dad's activities. Following that incident, I was afraid to stay in the room and the apartment, but I was more fearful that being with Dad would catch up with us and potentially have grave consequences.

# HEAD(LIGHTS)

The apartment complex had a basketball court, and the majority of the time, I was outside playing basketball by myself. Pretending to be Michael Jordan and Larry Bird, I played one-on-one and kept the score the entire game. Michael Jordan always won, but the game was close and usually down to the last second. I already played tackle football for our elementary school and decided that I wanted to play basketball. I knew Mom would be okay with it, so I got off the school bus excited. Something was different that day. I found my petite mother waiting for me, her blond hair parted down the middle in an 80s style, bearing an unusually stern expression in her hazel eyes.

"Can I try out for the basketball team?" I asked.

She shook her head as I spoke because she had other plans. When I looked past Mom into our car, three large black trash bags filled with our belongings were shoved in the back seat next to Jesse James.

"Get in the car," Mom cut me off, ruffling my hair. "We're moving to Ohio."

"Is Dad not coming?" I asked, with my eyes narrowing.

# JOHNN(Y)

After taking a long drag of her Marlboro Lights cigarette before stomping it out with her foot, she headed to the car. "Get in the car. We'll see him later."

I didn't understand what that meant, but leaving lifted a huge weight when I realized that burning down our home and everything about Dad was finally enough for Mom. I didn't know what was ahead, but at least my fate was no longer in his hands. That big jolt of fear I'd become accustomed to would diminish over time. We were finally leaving a less-than-idyllic childhood for something else.

We lived in Butcher Hollow until the end of the fall of my fourth-grade year. That gave me enough time to learn that a large part of Dad's problem was due to the opioid crisis. For him, like many others, there was no turning back. Oxy became the most abused drug. Unfortunately, addiction to Oxycodone pills was all too common. I never saw Dad do heroin or other drugs outside of marijuana after he started Oxy. Just those pills with different little numbers on them, and he couldn't stop.

The car had been making odd noises when Mom made a sharp detour on the way out of the Holler on

Route 23 outside of Paintsville, Kentucky. She pulled into a place where a rusted sign was hanging in the window that read "Garage." Junior, a guy a few years younger than Dad with a medium build, walked over, popped the hood, and began working on our car while Mom sent Jesse and I outside with a Cola. I'd never seen the guy before, but Mom seemed to know him pretty well. When Junior was finished, he told Mom to start the car, and then he jumped in the front seat next to her. He agreed to fix the car but wanted to go with us as part of the deal.

"What was wrong with it?" she asked.

"That damn Johnny secured the transmission by screwing two by fours into the engine!" Junior laughed. "This car wasn't makin' it to Oh-hi'a! Hell, it wasn't makin' it out the dadgum county!"

As we drove away, I watched the mountains fade with a sense of relief. A new journey was ahead of us.

# JOHNN(Y)

## FORGE • AHEAD

**THE NIGHT MY DAD** *walked past the headlights in front of the car is when I realized he was a completely different person. Even his appearance, walk, and demeanor as the lights shined on the barrel of his shotgun as he approached the trailer is a vivid memory that I've never managed to shake off.*

*Thinking back, I believe I just needed to see a light shining on our circumstances, but more importantly, my mom needed to see it. There were numerous times throughout our life that we could have seen the warning signs of how drugs took over my dad's life and even changed who he was. However, when you are stuck in a situation, it is hard to see what is truly happening. Many times, we dig in and persevere through the trauma because we don't know if we can survive outside of those circumstances. Sometimes, we are not even sure if there can be a life outside of what we know.*

*You could possibly be stuck in your own situation, where life hasn't gone exactly as planned and you're looking for a way out. My plea with you is this: do not wait for a headlight in your own life to illuminate the potential peril of your situation. Rather than it be drugs, abuse, anxiety, depression, or marital issues—see the warning signs ahead before your circumstances worsen.*

*Here are some common mental health warning signs that I believe my dad showed, symptoms that we started to see beaming in front of us that led to my mom's decision to leave:*

- **CHANGES IN MOOD**: *My dad seemed to always be moody and irritable, most of the time when he was not high.*

- **SOCIAL WITHDRAWAL**: *Over the years, my dad quit racing and being around his friends, which is most likely why he wasn't invited to the party in the first place.*

- **CHANGES IN APPETITE**: *My dad seemed to lose a lot of weight and didn't eat often as he started to take more drugs.*

- **HEIGHTENED ANXIETY**: My dad always had a fear of the police catching him and we often ran from the cops by traveling to different locations.
- **INCREASED SUBSTANCE ABUSE**: My dad relied on drugs to cope and deal with the day-to-day life in the holler.

The quicker you can realize the situation and seek help from your network while remaining steadfast in faith, the faster you can overcome your adversity and begin a life of healing and healthy relationships. I am thankful every day that my mom took my brother and me away from my father, as I would have most likely ended up a drug addict or worse, dead.

Mom, thank you.

# HEAD(LIGHTS)

# sun(glasses)

## JOHNN(IE)

**REGARDLESS OF PEOPLE'S PERCEPTIONS** of growing up in the hood, I was surrounded by some good guys—although it still seemed like we fought over everything. One of the kids who played two-hand touch football with us was Ben's cousin, Deion. We let Deion play because he always had a football. He wasn't the fastest, but Deion had the most wiggle of everybody—and the worst attitude. He'd take his little ball and leave if anyone tackled him too hard. And when Deion got mad because he didn't get a call that he thought he should, he'd punt the football out of the parking lot and walk away or try to fight.

The rest of us would laugh because we knew he'd be back to play the next time, and he'd most likely do the same thing. Although we got skinned and scraped up on that concrete because we were guaranteed to fall at some point, I loved playing football—we all did—and we knew that either football or basketball was the ticket out of here, so we wanted to be the best.

Mama wanted me to play basketball at William T. Dwyer, where she played. I was in elementary school, and during a game, in a packed gym, when they passed me the ball, I turned around and ran right up the court without dribbling or stopping, so they blew the whistle before I could shoot. Imagine that! It seemed I was better suited for football, so that's what I played. Football was fun, and it became a healthy outlet. I started playing at five years old and didn't want to stop.

I paid attention to what I was taught and started understanding the rules of football and the discipline that comes with playing. After that, my respect for the game was consistent, and that began to take shape in other areas of my life.

My first year of playing organized youth league football (and not just in the parking lot), I was on the

Riviera Beach Sharks team. I kept asking to play more and wanted to try different positions since it was my first time learning them, but the coach wouldn't give me a chance. I had my eye on playing running back, but the coach's son had that position, and his cousin was his backup. A coach that favors his blood was nothing new, but it felt unfair.

During the last game of the year, the coach had me play tight end. When they finally gave me the ball, it was the first time I'd touched it all season! The coach didn't know that playing ball with my cousins and friends over the years had really prepared me for that moment. I did a tight end reverse on the snap, came around, and ran into the endzone. It was then the coach realized I could be an asset to the team if they played me more the following season. It was a new high for me.

The following year, I had a different coach and more opportunities to play. I became one of the best players in the Little League system. I didn't want anyone else to block me from what I could show up and do out on the field, so it kept me digging in and getting better. The NFL dreams I had were possible because *I was good*. And if Devin Hester did it, I could too.

# SUN(GLASSES)

As kids, we don't always know the reality of grown folks' business, but that doesn't mean we don't respond to what we see or hear. Mama dealt with some tough situations when I was younger, and although I witnessed a few of the men hitting and pushing her, I was too young to know how to step in and help. I froze, scared. The inability to protect my mother made me feel helpless, and it also drove me to get her the hell out of any place where she could be hurt. I knew that I'd never put my hands on a woman; I learned that much for sure. Only a coward would do that.

Mama never said anything about what happened to her, and I didn't want to bring up anything that could be traumatizing for her to explain. I didn't know how she processed things or what she held inside, but her oversized shades let me know it was best to leave it alone. She didn't want me to see the damage. Mama wearing those black shades and extra dark lenses gave her the tool she needed to protect herself and maintain her emotional well-being. They shielded her from the harsh realities of life and kept her focused on what was truly significant. Looking through those lenses, she saw what was most important—me.

And although I never heard Grandma say anything around me, she was pissed when Mama pulled up wearing sunglasses—because she knew. Grandma and Auntie Shirley were the firecrackers of the siblings, and they didn't let anything slip past them.

My mother had an incredible work ethic and discipline, which set the bar for me. She didn't take the easy way out, make excuses, or give up. She never felt sorry for herself. That wasn't her. Maybe playing basketball had something to do with her attitude and dedication. She never complained about working at an old folk's home or anything she did. Sometimes she wasn't in the best mood after working all day, but I knew why and either would make Mama laugh or stay out of her way so she could rest.

My mother always seemed to find a way to provide for us. She was the one who made sure we had a home, food on the table, clothing, and everything we needed. She'd buy me Reeboks because they were nice but affordable, even though I was terrible with shoes. As soon as Mama bought me a pair, I was off playing football in them. They definitely didn't look new for long.

I appreciated everything Mama did for us, and I didn't complain about anything. Her struggle was real. As a kid, I didn't know everything she had to deal with to put food on the table, clothes on our backs, and keep a roof over our heads and the lights on. I knew that the last thing I wanted to be was a burden, but I wasn't completely aware of the sacrifices Mama was making for me. All I had to do was go to school, play football, help around the house a little, and be respectful. I knew things were tough financially since she was the sole provider, but if we didn't have something, Mama found a way to get it. And if I needed something, Mama or Grandma got it for me. I never had much, but it was enough. I didn't miss what we didn't have.

Despite how exhausted Mama was when she came home, with a tired but pleasant expression she'd still go into the kitchen and cook dinner. I'd walk into the house, and my mouth would start watering when I smelled her Oxtails with yellow rice and cabbage. Her meat pies were delicious, and she made the most tender and juicy pot roast in a bag, with mashed potatoes, corn, and celery—it smelled like dinner at church! And anyone who went to our church knew that was the best meal of the week, but it didn't beat Mama's pot roast!

That and everything she made was amazing! Mama would throw down on the souse she made from pork. She put every seasoning in the cabinet in it with a little mojo, vinegar, and potatoes, then she boiled it for nearly eight hours. Mama's souse was just so delicious! People used to drive around the hood selling their version of souse with hot sauce and crackers, but it wasn't even close to my mother's. After watching Mama and Grandma cook, I got fancy with egg sandwiches and other little things. I started experimenting with food more. Seeing Mama pour all that love into her food and having Grandma's good cooking caused me to develop my own passion for it. It was an escape from the outside world.

At nearly ten years old, I was just hitting the corner in my neighborhood, right behind my aunt's apartment, when I heard a loud *pop!* Gunfire. Just once, but I had no interest in knowing who was shooting or what was going on. I was cautious not to get into anything that wasn't my business, but the way the hood works, things happen inadvertently. I turned around and got up out of there. Another time, Mama, Ben, and I were at my grandmother's house in Stonybrook. Just as we got in the car to leave, someone started spraying bullets with an AK-47. Big bullets! The sound of those things scared me out of my mind. I didn't know where the shots were coming from or who was firing them, but Grandma came yelling for us to get back in the house.

The next day, we stopped by the candy lady's spot near Grandma's where we'd go in with a dollar and leave with a lot of candy. This time, there were bullet holes everywhere. My Aunt Shirley stayed in the apartment right next to them. The damage and size of the bullets made me realize that they were meant for someone, but they didn't have names on them. This was something we'd have to navigate and expect.

I didn't stay in the streets, so thankfully, I only heard gunshots a couple of times as a kid; there were also countless fights and drugs bought and sold, but I never felt like it was too crazy. The environment I grew up in had conditioned me, and I didn't see anything wrong with it or have the fear that others passing through may have had. I saw the hood differently because it was my home. My family and friends were there, and that was all I knew.

There were things I didn't need to know, so I never thought about them. Using or selling drugs wasn't my path. Others sold crack, coke, and weed, but I stayed away from it. Before addicts got really bad, they were like regular people, but eventually, they looked like zombies when they got deep into drugs. I saw the transformation over time, and it was sad.

We had a lot of different gangs in the hood and in middle school. It seemed like there were fights every day. Each gang had its own wall, and we knew what to avoid, but my cousin Fat Man would throw hands with anyone really quick. Fighting with them made me tougher, and being around them had a positive effect. I purposely filled my time playing football to avoid falling into anything else that would impede or stop my progress. I was one of the better kids on the team, playing receiver, running back, a little quarterback, and safety against other middle schools with one other kid from my hood, Ezra, or "E."

If I wasn't outside playing football or sleeping, I played Madden, Mortal Combat, Super Mario Bros.,

Donkey Kong, or other video games while snacking on hot sausages and blue, red, or green Sour Punch Straws I got at Mike's. Dreamcast was my first system, and I loved all those different little crazy, weird games.

When Ben was old enough, that boy wanted to go everywhere with me, especially since Mama was constantly working. If I didn't take him, he'd snitch. I suppose that was payback for the way I followed Tevia around. I shared a room with my brother, but it didn't bother me; we were barely in it. Besides twin beds, a television, and a PlayStation, we had all kinds of junk in our room. Shoes, socks, and our stuff were everywhere.

In middle school, I had a fathead of Devin Hester on my wall, and I kept it throughout high school. Wherever we moved, that fathead moved, too, because it was motivation to keep me on a straight path and my mind on football. He was the greatest kick returner. He went to Suncoast High School and was related to my Aunt Linda's husband. When I was a sixth-grader, Devin signed my flag football jersey and shook my hand.

I told Mama, "I'm never washing my hand again," and I didn't that whole day.

Devin was the first person to return an opening kick in a Super Bowl. He made me want to be a kick returner, too, though it's hard to fill shoes like that.

Tevia moved in with us at Venetian Isles in Lake Park. It was only a few miles from Stonybrook. We kept the house tidy, washed dishes, and took care of Ben when Mama was working. Mama didn't demand anything other than that we clean our rooms and take out meat to thaw if she was cooking when she got home.

Grandma got sick, and one day she fell down the stairs and broke her hip. She stayed with my uncle for a little bit and then with us in Lake Park for a significant amount of time. I was grateful that I could be around her more, but she was slowly getting worse. Grandma was constantly coughing and wasn't as mean, but she was still Grandma. Before she became seriously ill, we started attending church together. She seemed to be in a peaceful place, especially since she'd given her life to God in her last year. The changes in Grandma stayed with me. Grandma wasn't as strong as before she fell, but she still managed to get up and praise God in church. Needless to say, that didn't last long; eventually, she was placed in hospice.

Everything changed when I turned 13. I lost my best friend and her unconditional love when Grandma passed. She was only 51 years young.

One afternoon, Mama visited Grandma. Shortly after, my Aunt Soya came to pick up Tevia and me. She took us to see Grandma; somehow, I knew she was gone. It was painful losing my grandmother. What made it worse was that I didn't have the chance to say goodbye, tell her how much I loved her, or explain her impact on my life. Good people always leave an impact. When I walked into her room, I heard the sobs and crying from all my family members surrounding her bed. It broke my heart when I slipped between them; my eyes rested on Grandma lying there, stiller and more peaceful than I'd ever seen her. Devastated, I collapsed to the ground, crying harder than I ever had. Losing Grandma so early in life affected me greatly. It was my first time seeing someone close to me pass, and it was rough.

With Grandma gone, I had several moments of reflection, but my way of dealing was pouring everything I had into the sport I loved. That was the only way I knew how to work through the pain and tremendous loss. Football gave me an outlet.

Football also taught me that I wanted to be someone people could count on, and high school would be the test.

# SUN(GLASSES)

## FORGE • AHEAD

**WE KNEW ADVERSITY HAD** hit whenever Mama showed up wearing those oversized sunglasses. The sun was always bright, but even on cloudy days, she wore them to hide the previous night's pain. Just as those sunglasses concealed Mama's bruised eye, I often wore sunglasses to shield my eyes from the sun's glare reflecting off the ocean's surface. The ocean reminded me a lot of Mama's struggles; on the surface, I saw the beauty of the waves. The calming sound of her voice reminded me of the waves at night, soothing and peaceful. But an entirely different world existed below the surface, unseen from the shores. In some way, we all have coping mechanisms and strategies to protect ourselves from life's emotional pain and discomfort.

Mama wearing those black shades and extra dark lenses gave her the tool she needed to protect herself and maintain her emotional well-being. They shielded her from the harsh realities of life and kept her focused on what was *truly significant. Looking through those lenses, she saw what was most important—me.*

*We often have a coping mechanism we hide behind regarding mental health. Similar to wearing sunglasses, we can hide behind substance abuse, avoidance, isolation, overworking, emotional eating, self-harm, escapism, or perfectionism. The good news? There are ways to overcome these hurdles, beginning with a healthy mindset. Here are five steps to overcome your coping mechanisms:*

- **RECOGNIZE**: *Acknowledge and accept that these coping mechanisms are not sustainable or healthy in the long-term.*

- **SEEK SUPPORT**: *Reach out to trusted friends, family members, or mental health professionals for support and guidance.*

- **DEVELOP HEALTHY COPING STRATEGIES**: *Explore healthier ways to cope with stress and manage emotions, such as mindfulness, exercise, therapy, or creative outlets.*

- **CREATE A SUPPORTIVE NETWORK**: *Surround yourself with supportive individuals or a church, who understand your struggles and encourage positive change.*

- **PRACTICE SELF-LOVE:** *Be kind to yourself and recognize that overcoming these coping mechanisms takes time and effort.*

*There are so many people who love you and want you to become your best self. Instead of relying on your current coping mechanisms, make a change and develop a new strategy while becoming vulnerable with yourself. Remove the veil and seek the foundation you need for a mentally healthy life!*

*Mama, thank you.*

# floor(joist)

## JOHNN(Y)

IN KENTUCKY, I LEARNED their version of the three Rs: reading, righting, and Route 23. I'd always heard that the best thing to do was travel north on Route 23 and get out of Kentucky because there was nothing there, so that's what Mom did that day. She heard about available manufacturing jobs and opportunities for a better life. Coal mining was dead. Mom wanted something more, and she didn't want us to fall into the same life as our father.

But the mountains, hills, and overall landscape were majestic and had become my refuge, part of home that I'd miss. Ohio was nothing more than corn fields as far as the eye could see. It was a vastly different environment than I was used to. Where I was from, we didn't say "creek," we said "crick;" "soda" or "pop" was called "Cola."

Being with our grandparents placed us in an encouraging environment, with more opportunities for Mom and us. My grandparents had always provided healthy emotional support, guidance, and exposure to a better way of life, and we needed it. I wished I didn't have to go to the Salvation Army for clothing and look for shoes that didn't have holes, but I was grateful I had clothes at all. The reality is that I experienced poverty for most of my adolescence. Circleville presented another option to us: exposure to something grander. The world is bigger than the environment Dad placed us in, and it's more expansive than what my mind had been accepting.

The summer after we left the Holler, Dad called Mom and told her he wanted to see his kids. My grandparents took us shopping and bought us brand new clothes to wear while we were with Dad. Mom took Jesse and I back to the Holler and dropped us off for a couple of weeks.

Dad lived in a small travel camper at the racetrack. It wasn't much, but it never was. The entire time we were with him, Dad had me shoveling horse manure, putting straw in the stalls, and helping him around the track. If there was a dirt race at night, he ran the water truck to give the cars better traction and minimize the dust. The track had a problem with groundhogs, and Dad showed me how to use his .22 rifle for hunting them. I'd find an empty horse stall and hide under the hay, watching along the base of the cliff overhang where I saw the groundhogs had dug holes. They typically came out right before sunset scavenging for food along the base of the mountain. I'd sit patiently for hours until one popped out of his hole, unaware that I was waiting. Staring through the scope, my breathing and heart rate increased. Finally, I'd steady my breath, flick the safety off, and *bang!*

The racetrack manager paid me $2.00 for every groundhog I shot. And since Dad never went to the store, I used the money to buy food and snacks from the concession stand during the race.

When Mom picked us up, Jesse and I stood in front of her looking shabby and unkempt, wearing the same clothing we had on when she dropped us off. Dad had taken and sold all of our new clothes for drug money.

"What did you do?" She shook her head in disbelief after I told her, a cigarette dangling from her mouth. "You're not coming back here!"

Knowing Mom meant what she said, I focused on my life in Circleville. During my fifth-grade year, my father came to visit; Grandpa was less tolerant of how he treated us and had the sheriff pick Dad up before he saw us. They escorted him to the Kentucky border and dropped him off, warning Dad that they'd throw him in prison for the rest of his life if he ever returned to Ohio.

Dad never came back.

---

SHORTLY AFTER MOVING TO Ohio, Mom began dating and eventually married my stepdad, Keith. She never withdrew her love from my brother and me; however, I had some resentment because I never saw Dad again, plus Mom spent most of her time with her husband rather than with us. While it wasn't possible to understand the gravity of his addiction at that point, it wasn't hard to tell that Dad wasn't a good person. Settling into a completely different environment was the best thing for all of us.

Unfortunately, it wasn't long before Keith started taking his problems out on Mom. Dad had his issues, but I never saw him lay a hand on Mom. I was angry that she let my stepdad get away with hurting her physically. One night, I was lying on the floor, Jesse asleep on the couch, when they came home from the bar next door. My stepdad followed Mom into their bedroom, and they argued while I tried blocking out the yelling with my pillow. Mom was cussing when I heard a loud pop.

"You mother f—r, you just broke my nose!" Mom shouted angrily. When she stormed out of the room, stepping over me, I pretended to be asleep but peeked from under my pillow to see blood draining from her nose. I already knew what it was like to be afraid of my environment, and that moment caused me to fear what someone could do.

The popular groups in high school, made up of athletes and the more affluent kids in the city, were accepting of me, probably because I lived with my grandparents most of the time. When my friends came over, they came to my grandparents' home. Grandma always kept the house decorated nicely, and I think it created the illusion that I lived far better than I actually did, increasing my popularity. I rarely invited friends to our apartment.

There was a time that Mom asked if I was embarrassed by her and my stepdad. She locked eyes with me, searching for the truth. But that wasn't the case. In Circleville, there were the "haves" and "have nots," and I didn't think I could fit in with the "haves" if they knew the truth. My grandparents had that success, not us. I told my friends I lived with my grandparents, but it wasn't because I was ashamed; it's where I spent most of my time and where I fit in.

I adapted rather quickly and hanging out with my grandparents helped. I was used to having freedom in the woods, so I rode my bike four miles to school every day unless it was raining or too cold, then Grandpa would drive me. My deep Appalachian dialect was unique to the kids, and there was no way to disguise it or hide the smell of Marlboro embedded in my clothes, a scent that kids usually teased me about. Mom and my stepdad were chain smokers, so the only fresh air was outside. Regardless of my clothing, dialect, and being a "have not", when they met Johnny Wayne, despite the name, they met the real me, authentic and genuinely outgoing.

Once I started meeting kids and making friends when I was a little older, I adopted a process that helped me maintain a good group of friends—I introduced them to my grandmother first. I felt she was a wise judge of character. If she didn't like someone, I didn't hang around with them. But when she approved of someone, I didn't care what my parents thought about them. Some of the kids Grandma was concerned about proved she had good reason. They became negative influences on others and eventually used or sold drugs. Her opinion mattered most. Our relationship was the strongest and a testament to how I'd turn out. Come hell or high water, Grandma had my back.

I stayed relatively active and loved rollerblading around Circleville. I thought it was safe, and nobody bothered me until I was thirteen. I didn't have a lot, but I had on a nice Steelers Starter jacket until a black Chevy pulled over, cutting me off in a church parking lot. Three kids hopped out of the car and made me take off my jacket and give it to them. One of them shouted, "If you don't—we're gonna kick your ass!"

---

THE HOUSE MY GRANDPARENTS owned was a grand Victorian style. Before they bought it, it was a large funeral home and a stop on the underground railroad when several stations were active. My grandfather told me stories and said under the basement, there used to be a tunnel that extended out to the Scioto River. The tunnel was used to help slaves continue to migrate north along the Scioto River away from danger. It was under the staircase and behind the water heater and furnace. He warned me not to go down there. Curious, I jumped into the tunnel and started to crawl a few feet, but the tunnel had collapsed. Disappointed, I crawled out of the tunnel, slid past the water heater and furnace, then poked my head out behind the staircase, and there stood Grandpa.

"Where ya been?" he asked.

"Uh, checking out the tunnel," I replied.

"Well, I guess I'm going to have to fill it with concrete," Grandpa said. He made me his laborer to help him with the concrete as punishment.

Grandpa's basement was my favorite place to hang out as I got older. There was a billiards room with a monochrome floor, and a bar with a Budweiser sign on the wall behind it.

I'd ask Grandma if I could have a few friends over, and while she'd give me permission, a few usually turned into about 30 or more 15- and 16-year-old kids. The funny thing is that Grandma didn't mind, but she had concerns. She told me that my friends had access to alcohol, and if someone got drunk, left her home, and got hurt, we were liable. My actions affected them. In everything I did, she wanted me to be mindful of my actions—they could cost someone their life. Grandma had a way of making me understand and consider the outcome of my decisions and actions, which was something I had never been taught.

She'd say, "One action leads to another," and I held onto her words.

Grandma's calming demeanor got through to me. She used it to have some of the most effective yet gentle conversations, coupled with profound insight. Knowing who she was made me never want to upset or disappoint her. I wanted my grandmother to be proud of me. Even when I did something bad, without raising her voice she'd make me understand what I did was wrong and then offer another option. She'd often start by saying, "Have you thought of..." Anytime I heard her lead with that phrase, I knew I had messed up and was about to learn a different approach.

I appreciated Grandma's constant guidance, especially since my parents' tactics were less impactful. They just yelled at me. After a while, it became ineffective, and I got used to it. I valued Grandma's method of raising me and making me a better young man.

Grandma and Mom always gave me lunch money, but beginning in October, I had other plans for it. Instead, I'd grab a snack from the pantry and save every penny I could manage, stuffing the money into a pair of shoes I never wore. A few days before Christmas, I went to the Dollar Store and bought Grandma and Mom a present. I bought both of them a mirror with a scene of baby Jesus. There were decorative little white ivory figurines that she could set up on the mirror. When I gave it to Grandma that Christmas, she kept it forever.

Every Christmas Eve, my grandparents made it a big festive event, inviting all my aunts, uncles, and cousins—about 30 to 40 people in total—to dinner. Grandma cooked all day long: deviled eggs, celery stuffed with cream cheese, glazed ham, a green bean casserole, mashed potatoes, pies, and other desserts. It was a feast! The men went to the bar or hung out in the basement, played pool, and drank. The grandkids hung out together, and the women sat and talked because Grandma always had everything ready.

Grandma loved cooking and baking. She'd always set the table, and everything was on it: side dishes, main dishes, and delicious desserts. Eating together that way was unfamiliar to me, and the only time I experienced it was with my grandparents. They'd talk about their day and ask about my day at school. Anywhere we lived in the Holler, the table was never big enough to sit around, and half the time we didn't have a table. I'd get my food and eat on the couch or sit on the floor.

Grandma seemed to know what I needed because our relationship was unique. We'd prank each other all the time. She taught me how to wash dishes, and I loved doing dishes with her, especially using the spray nozzle. I'd take a hairband, attach it to the sprayer, and point it at her. When the water turned on, I soaked her. She'd yelp every time and say, "You little son of a gun, I'm getting you back!"

Grandma was strawberry blonde and 5'3", with infectious laughter and water dripping down her face. She'd always try to get me back by scaring me, jumping out from around a corner or somewhere when I didn't expect it. Grandma did that from the time I was a little kid to high school, when she was 65 years young.

My grandmother wasn't without her share of adversity. She overcame a great deal to be the kind of person she was, and anyone who didn't know her story wouldn't hear it from her. My grandmother's father and grandfather worked on the railroad. They drank heavily, and every time they did, she and her sisters moved a dresser in front of the door so they wouldn't get abused. When she was 13, her parents sold her to a guy in Corbin, Kentucky.

Grandma didn't graduate from high school, but she managed to get away from the man who bought her, and she married Grandpa. Together, they had two boys and three girls, including Mom. They were together for a long time until separating due to Grandpa's heavy hand when it came to Grandma and his children. Years later, they reconciled, and I only knew my grandparents by how they treated me.

Grandma's parenting style was to let her kids do what they wanted and figure it out as they went. Maybe that's where Mom adopted her parenting style. But Grandma was vastly different with me. Apparently, Grandma had changed over time.

Mom and Keith took me to Goodwin's Family Restaurant when I was 12; that was the first sit-down restaurant we ate at as a family. They had smoking and non-smoking sections, and since they both smoked, we sat in the smoking section that looked like mornings in the Holler. My eyes scanned the menu with excitement, and when the waitress asked what I wanted, I got what sounded good. I didn't understand what it would cost them, and they didn't tell me what I couldn't order. Unfortunately, getting a meal that was $12.00 upset my stepdad, and he reprimanded me so severely that I couldn't enjoy it.

# FLOOR(JOIST)

Having a stepdad was an adjustment. I had more freedom in the Holler because no one really watched me; I looked after Dad. Even though we left the Holler, my habits from back home crept into my daily life without me realizing it. We were sitting on a couch in our tiny apartment above my grandparents' house watching TV's Bloopers & Practical Jokes.

After watching a guy flip over the handlebars of his bike and crash into the ground, I said, "Oh man, that guy's screwed!"

"Don't you ever use that language again!" my stepdad shouted angrily.

After seeing how Keith treated Mom, I quickly became afraid of him. I didn't want him to treat me that way. It didn't make sense that we moved from one unsafe environment to another. I didn't like being placed in that situation, but I didn't have a choice.

Although I saw Mom and my stepdad after work, they didn't stick around long. They routinely did their own thing and ventured out to the bar more often than not. I stayed with my grandparents for the first two years. Then, my parents rented an 800 square foot baby blue house with an alley behind it and a field next to us on Hayward Street. Entering through the front door, there was a tiny living room to the left, a small dining area off the kitchen on the right, a bathroom down the hall, and my parents' room on the left. Jesse and I shared a room on the right. Even though there was nothing in our room besides a mattress, I felt my parents were doing better. That first night, I sat in the living room and watched *The Mask* with Jesse. Once we got settled, I started building model cars on the weekends while listening to Aerosmith's "Get a Grip" when I wasn't working with my stepdad.

My stepdad framed homes for a big company. He also had a side job building custom sheds and pole barns that he would make me help with, starting around 12 years old. On the weekends, he woke me up before six each morning; it was always dark when we left to build sheds. It seemed we always had a job in the middle of nowhere, so we had to leave early to get to the worksite. He had an old red Ford truck with a utility bed and a roof rack. He'd smoke cigarettes with the windows rolled down, no matter how cold it was. There were many occasions when I was freezing while in the truck with him, but the crisp morning air woke me every time. I was responsible for ensuring the air compressor, extension cords, and materials needed to build sheds were on his truck.

He'd say, "We're not leaving 'til it's done," so I worked harder and faster. I'd take out the wood, organize it, get the air compressor hooked up, and connect extension cords to the saws. I did a lot of work just getting him ready.

I was 11 when I started. By the time I was 14, he had taught me how to use a saw. He'd read off the measurements, and I'd cut all day. He'd say, "I need ten two-by-fours, 92 inches long," and I'd cut them. There wasn't much I couldn't do. He told me to cut the wood to build a wall while he went to the gas station. I took a nail gun, put it together, and had the wall built by the time he returned. For the first few years, he didn't pay me anything. When I finally spoke up and told him, "You need to start paying me," he knew I'd earned it, so he paid me five dollars an hour. I worked hard and never complained.

My stepdad gave me *Rich Dad Poor Dad*, which was his way of encouraging me to learn how to be a rich dad. Although he didn't make much money, he did the best he could to provide for us and worked extremely hard. I learned a lot about values and work ethic, but my parents never escaped poverty because of a lack of financial literacy.

In the winter, my stepdad and I were framing a house and we had to put wood on the floor joists, but they had frosted over. Beneath me was a beam holding up the freshly poured concrete walls for the basement. I slipped on a joist and fell ten feet through the basement onto iced gravel! A two-by-four holding up the wall went straight into my ribs and snapped in two while my face was planted in gravel. The pain was excruciating!

With a cigarette dangling from his mouth, the frigid air created a white cloud as he looked and yelled, "What the damn hell are you doing boy?! Get out of the basement! We've got work to do!"

"I—I—I can't—"

"Dammit! Suck it up and go hook up the generator!"

Laying on the cold frozen gravel underneath the floor joist was a harsh lesson. On the one hand, I wanted my stepfather to jump down and console me. I wanted him to understand the pain I felt and tell me I was going to be okay. On the other hand, I'm glad he didn't. I didn't know then, but he built my foundation by forcing me to overcome the adversity I faced. He could tell if I was hurt badly, or at least I hoped he would.

He wasn't any other way than tough on me, but in the process, he taught me how to build sheds, frame houses, and create something. Inadvertently, he taught me to be patient with others and strict with myself. I did framing with him until I was 18, but that particular moment prepared me to be a hard but effective leader. Oh, it hurt like hell, but without saying a word, I got up and went back to work, mentally pushing past the pain. And after that, for some reason or another, I believed I could get through anything.

## FORGE • AHEAD

**IRONICALLY, THE VERY THING** I slipped on was the same thing that represents the support and structure of a house, like that in our own lives. A foundation represents the fundamental things we need to survive and thrive. Our floor joist serves as the foundation we need to create a fulfilling life. Just as a house cannot stand without a strong floor joist, we also need support and structure to pursue our goals and dreams.

Although floor joists are unseen and hidden beneath the surface, they are sources of support: the love and encouragement of family and friends, our inner resilience found through faith and purpose. They are reminders that we can get through anything, even when the world tries to crumble our foundation. The foundation is often the first piece of construction; as parents, grandparents, aunts and uncles, and even youth coaches, we have the ability to create a strong mental foundation within our youth as they face an ever-changing and challenging social world.

Teaching our youth foundational principles for cultivating a strong mindset can lay the groundwork for their own mental floor joist. Here are five key principles for helping our youth and each other:

- **SELF-AWARENESS**: Encourage youth you encounter to recognize and understand their emotions, thoughts, and behaviors.

- **RESILIENCE**: Teach them that setbacks and challenges are a natural part of life and that they have the ability to bounce back from adversity. Encourage them to view their failures as opportunities while learning from their mistakes.

- **POSITIVE SELF-TALK**: Promote self-esteem and self-confidence by highlighting their strengths and talents. Help them create phrases to tell themselves each morning to build confidence.

- **EMOTIONAL REGULATION**: Help children develop strategies for managing their emotions constructively. Teach them relaxation techniques, mindfulness exercises, or deep breathing to calm themselves when feeling overwhelmed or upset.

- **SOCIAL CONNECTION**: *Emphasize the importance of supportive relationships and encourage children to cultivate strong connections with family, friends, and trusted adults. Teach them effective communication skills and empathy to foster healthy relationships while seeking support when needed.*

*By instilling these principles from an early age, children can develop the resilience, self-awareness, and emotional intelligence needed to navigate life's challenges while maintaining a positive mindset.*

*The day I slipped on that frost-covered two-inch by eight-inch floor joist and fell into the basement, fighting through labored breathing, is the day I began constructing my foundation. Unfortunately, I had to learn the hard way, but you have a choice today to begin building the foundation in your own life to withstand the adversities many of us face. We all have life experiences to reflect upon that can help us create a stronger foundation, so dig deep.*

*Keith, thank you.*

# FLOOR(JOIST)

# bridge(s)

## JOHNN(IE)

**WE MOVED TO THIRD** Street in Jupiter, Florida, and I began ninth grade at Cardinal Newman High School in West Palm Beach. It was the first time we had a house of our own, complete with a garage. My mom was still working hard to provide for us and give us a good life.

As a kid, I had no choice but to attend church, and I'm appreciative that Mama and Grandma built that foundation. In high school, I had a little more freedom with some of my choices and didn't feel attending church was the only way to get the Word I needed from God. Since my relationship with God was vital, I decided that He could hear me wherever I was. If that was in the middle of practice on the field, that's where I'd pray.

95

And I did. When coaches or kids asked what I was doing, I'd tell them, "I'm praying. Leave me alone."

Internally, I was humble. I still went to church when I needed the Word on a different level, but whether I was in church or not, I wouldn't part with God because my life depended on my faith.

I played football and basketball, the two sports I'd always participated in, but shortly after the football season ended, I transferred to Dwyer. In my heart, I knew Cardinal Newman wasn't where I belonged. I was aware I could've been better at football, and I didn't know how to navigate to that next level, where coaches and scouts would notice my talent. The environment at Cardinal Newman wasn't feeding my goals, and that didn't sit right with me.

I needed proper coaching and encouragement to help me continue developing, and I was hungry to be the best player I could be. Football was my way out of the hood, and from what I could tell, it appeared to be my only way out. Every year I kept getting better and better, which showed me what was possible with discipline and commitment.

# JOHNN(IE)

Since my mother attended Dwyer, she knew about the danger and didn't want me to get caught up in the hood part of the school. I had no reason not to trust Mama, so I avoided mischief as much as possible. I still saw the typical fights and navigated away from gangs and other bad situations, but I got along with most people—being an athlete made it easier. I saw less violence there than what I grew up with, which may have been because I barely made it to parties. Instead, I stayed at the crib, went bowling with the homies, or hung out with my girl.

Every time I ran track or headed to P.E., I saw Mama's name on the track and football stadium walkway. It was cool and inspiring at the same time. I arrived at Dwyer just as track began, but as a transfer, I wasn't eligible to run that season. Still, it worked out because I played spring ball that year and made a name for myself on the field. People took notice of my skills. Given all I did was play football, playing year-round was natural. I was headed in a clear direction.

After that year, when football season ended, I ran track—the 100-meter dash, 200-meter dash, 4x100-meter relay, and 4x400-meter relay. Track was vital to excelling in football. As a receiver, explosiveness was a requirement. As a sprinter, it gave me an edge to have a higher level of adaptability.

Having the right coaches at Dwyer who instinctively knew how to push me to the next level helped me make a substantial jump to an entirely different kind of player. I didn't stop getting better; I kept turning it up! Mama stayed on me about my grades. I got As and Bs throughout middle school, and I continued to do well in high school.

High school was smooth sailing and fun. At one point, I told my mom I wanted to go to culinary school and I also wanted to act. But I couldn't do those things and play football, so I missed out on developing those skills and exploring those paths. I knew the sacrifice was going to be worth it, though.

Although I was still one to have fun, "Little Bad Ass Johnnie" had long resigned, and a whole new passion and purpose for football emerged. Our team did pretty well due to our talent, discipline, and excellent coaching and leadership. Mama was at all of my games. I also started seeing more of Pops. He would show up for most of my games and bring friends with him, as though he was showing me off and proud of me.

By this time, I realized that everybody knew Pops and he was the most popular person I'd ever known. We didn't have much of a relationship early on, but I always admired him. I only saw him happy and making jokes. If Pops had a bad day, it wasn't around me. We started bowling here and there, which helped me get to know him a little better. Pops was rather good at bowling, and he even kicked my butt a few times.

When I looked in the stands at the start of our games, Pops was at most of them. We always dapped up and hugged when we saw each other, and he'd grab my head and call me "J Baby!"

My dad didn't know how to be a dad in those early, formative years. Perhaps he didn't have the mentorship growing up to be what he could be as a father, but football bonded us. Besides, I was grateful to have good coaches around me to fill in the gaps. Plus, I always had the support of the communities I was in. They wanted to see me succeed.

We had a successful season at Dwyer, and what made it extra special was that Ezra, the boy I played football with growing up and who is still one of my best friends today, was also a part of the journey to the championship game. The amount of natural talent the two of us brought to represent our neighborhood was unreal, even if our run didn't end the way we hoped. In the game before the state championship, I dropped a critical pass on fourth and eight. I took it hard, but my passion and discipline for the game took me right back to work the next day. Without pause, I began training in preparation for the upcoming season. I found that there's always something pushing me one way or another, and that loss turned me into a whole different animal.

The safeties coach was also the track coach for sprinters, so I got him in double doses. He had us running across the long Florida bridges in the scorching heat. Then, acknowledging how bad it was, he finally told us we were done and wouldn't have to run across those bridges anymore. However, out of nowhere the next week when we were already soaked in sweat on a dangerously sweltering day, he told us to get to running down the bridge again. I knew it was stupid to have a bunch of kids run the bridges in those temperatures after he told us we wouldn't do it again. *So I quit.*

That didn't last because as soon as the football head coach Jack Daniels heard about it, he made me return.

Coach Daniels began mentoring and working with me in a way that helped me change my perspective on my personal growth. If he addressed something, I listened. Coach Daniels cared about the path we were on as young men. He sat his team down and ripped us up like nothing I'd ever seen from a coach, but it was also constructive criticism. He told us what we were doing wrong, why, and how to fix it.

One time, Coach Daniels pointed at me and said, "You ain't got no character!"

"What?"

Looking directly into my narrowing eyes, he repeated it purposely giving me a moment to digest his intent. "You ain't got no character."

He jarred me. I had no clue what he meant, but it resonated with me so deeply that I asked people what having a lack of character meant. I had to dig down and figure out what he was talking about because he was never wrong. Then it hit me hard. I might have grown out of "Badass Little Johnnie," but I was now the class clown. He meant he knew I could be something special, but I was blowing it by being the goofy one who would get in trouble. I couldn't be a leader on the field without being one in other areas of my life, so I had to learn to exude leadership consistently. It took time, but I worked toward being an undeniable leader because Coach Daniels recognized something different in me. It was more than what I saw in myself.

Coach Daniels didn't just point things out and let us deal with the consequences if we didn't work toward personal growth. We listened to and respected him because he told us *why* it was necessary to change and *why* we needed to be concerned about the direction of our lives. Most people had their own lives and problems to manage. They didn't have time or interest in mentoring, or even caring, about kids who weren't theirs—particularly young black kids from the hood labeled with little hope for a successful future. The difference was that Coach Daniels cared enough to pay attention to our actions and character, and pointed out our blind spots.

Knowing that we were leaving in a few years, he could've coached us and left everything else alone, especially since he had new kids coming in every season. Coach Daniels could have kept his focus on nothing but football; however, that wasn't his objective. He declined to take that route and chose to become a father figure to many of us who didn't have one or needed a little extra guidance. But more importantly, Coach Daniels understood the need to invest in us and help shape our mindset beyond football. He was aware that all we saw was what was in front of us, but the bigger picture was most important: there is life outside of football, and we are more than just football players. At that time, he wanted more for us than we could see for ourselves, and he pushed us because he knew it was achievable.

After Coach Daniels brought the revelation about my character to my attention, the changes started. I gained a different perspective on nearly everything. Scouts asked our high school teachers and coaches how we were as students, what our grades were, and other questions to determine if we were a leader. My future success in accomplishing my dreams wasn't just about my performance on the field; it was combined with my character and behavior in life. My relationships and who I aligned myself with came full circle. Sometimes a change of perspective is what we need. It can give us the tools to accomplish the exact things we're trying to do.

Through the coaching and consistent guidance I received, I changed and became fully committed to my goals. Nothing or no one could impede my progress. I was learning that regardless of the adversity we are faced with or surrounded by, we have a choice to do better, to be better, and reach beyond the expectations of others. Mentally, I had to wrap my mind around that possibility, and I needed to see it visually. Every season was an opportunity to improve in several areas, and in the tenth grade, I went hard at my goals, knowing everything about my future could be decided in every performance.

However, in just five seconds on the field, everything changed. We were playing seven-on-seven during the 2011-2012 season. I took off down the field, hitting the go route hard. I felt a grip on the back of my collar, an illegal pull that twisted me mid-stride. Time seemed to slow as I tumbled, my legs folding underneath me in an awkward tangle that felt like being wrapped up in knots. Lying there on the turf, I could feel the sharp sting in both knees, a pain that was more than physical—it was the ache of my future hanging in the balance. It meant sitting out the next seven-on-seven, watching from the sidelines when I knew every play counted. College scouts were starting to take notice, and time was ticking—each game, each play, could be the difference. I was barely a step away from making it to college ball, and an injury was the last thing I needed on my path.

Although injuries in football are inevitable, putting things on "pause" due to an injury was unfathomable. My whole life was wrapped up in a future where I played football in college and professionally. There was nothing else—so I kept pushing, pushing, pushing through the pain. My mom was counting on me.

# BRIDGE(S)

## FORGE • AHEAD

**RUNNING ACROSS THOSE BRIDGES** in the Florida heat was the hardest level of training I committed to in high school. We were dripping sweat from the humidity before we even started! The heat from the concrete crept through my shoes, and I felt the burn with every step. Coach wanted us to know that we were doing something hard, and it would only get more difficult. Mentally, if we ran until he told us to stop, we could make it. However, when our coach told us we were done and decided to make us continue, it forced us to build our own bridge of resilience. Our minds instantly gave up when he said that we were finished, as you always give up mentally before you do physically.

Bridges are built to connect us over obstacles and reach our destination. They are designed to withstand any weather condition and must remain strong and resilient. Our coach was helping each of us understand how we were creating a bridge for our mindset. But at the moment, I resented our coach for making us continue. Oftentimes we will hold resentment towards those who affect our mental health without a way to connect and build a bridge to rekindle a healthy relationship. Building a bridge with someone who is causing you mental health harm can be particularly challenging and may create even more damage, but it is often necessary to build a bridge with that individual for your own well-being. Here are a few suggestions to consider:

- **SET BOUNDARIES**: Clearly communicate your boundaries with the individual, discussing which behavior you perceive to be acceptable and how you expect to be treated.

- **EXPRESS YOUR FEELINGS**: It's ok to be vulnerable; if they genuinely care, they'll listen. Calmly and assertively express how their actions or words are affecting your mental health.

- **SEEK MEDIATION**: If necessary, involve a neutral third party, such as a therapist or mediator, to facilitate a constructive dialogue and help find common ground.

- **FOCUS ON SOLUTIONS**: Use the E+R=O mindset; instead of dwelling on past outcomes, focus on finding new solutions and strategies for improving the relationship moving forward.

- **KNOW WHEN TO WALK AWAY**: Ultimately, if efforts to reconcile prove to remain toxic despite your best efforts, it may be time to distance yourself for the sake of your own mental health.

I am thankful Coach Daniels had the foresight and leadership to establish a bridge with me after I quit. He knew that my mental health bridge was in progress and ensured that these critical conversations continued as he was instilled values only he knew I had.

Coach Daniels, thank you.

# sand(fleas)

## JOHNN(Y)

AT THE AGE OF 15, I wanted to enlist in the Army until my best friend Trevor and I watched *The Rock* with Sean Connery.

"Why are you trying to enlist in the Army?" he asked. I shrugged. He continued, "The Marines are the hardest and most elite military in the world! The Army?"

After some research and thinking about it, I decided I could become a Marine. I read *White Feather*, a widely recognized propaganda symbol representing cowardice or conscientious pacifism. Carlos Hathcock was one of the deadliest snipers in Vietnam. After reading his memoir, I knew that's what I wanted to do. The nature of his presence protecting the men around him was appealing. The Marine Corps is a tight knit brotherhood. Hathcock was sought after as a guardian angel because he looked over the Marines in Vietnam. I admired how he approached the craft of being a sniper and the mental fortitude it must have taken for him to do the things he had to do.

As with the rest of our country, the tragic occurrences of 9/11 were pivotal. I was sitting in Mr. Hunter's English class when a chuckle came from the back of the room, where Mr. Hunter was on his computer. Then, he told the class, "Someone just bombed the Pentagon."

I asked, "Why would you laugh?" but he didn't respond.

A teacher rolled in a gray old-style tube TV soon after. Collectively, the entire class watched in terror as the second plane hit the twin towers.

The occurrences on that tragic day impacted me significantly and contributed to why I needed to be a part of our military. The world watched as the towers came down, and I witnessed the fear and devastation it caused. Yet we, this country, came together as one body of people—something I'd never seen in my generation.

The day after 9/11 may be one of the saddest and greatest days this Nation has seen. We didn't bicker or care about our differences; instead, on September 12th, we understood the power of unity. The twin towers weren't just two buildings. They symbolized strength, unity, and a representation of what America stood for, side by side. In the footage of people running for their lives, the only color anyone could see was gray from the ash that covered everyone in the vicinity. When those towers fell, politics and opinions fell with them for a brief period. However, fundamental respect for each other as humans, regardless of background, race, culture, or economic status, was all we knew and what we relied on.

The unity I felt at that moment was unforgettable. Nothing could motivate me more to become a United States Marine than watching innocent people jump from the windows of the fiery twin towers. Then, I started realizing everything was bigger than me. The freedoms we have in this Nation are for everyone who comes here, and they should be able to feel free from tyranny. Once I started possessing a military mindset, I was immensely proud of our Nation and had a sense of pride in being an American. Feeling my share of the burden to continue that mission of unity, I decided to enlist in the Marine Corps as soon as possible, at 17.

I needed Mom to sign me up for the Delayed Entry Program (DEP) or else I'd have to wait until I graduated.

"Either you sign the paperwork and I come home and visit, or I sign it at 18 and you'll never see me again," I told her. Reluctantly, she signed. Fully committed and self-disciplined, I trained with the other recruits and independently as though I was enlisting the following day, running three to five miles daily, even across flooded fields while saddled with a weighted backpack. I believed the harder I trained on my own, the easier boot camp would be. I regularly lifted for hours at a time. By my senior year, I had a solid training regimen and was ready for my journey. Mentally, physically, and emotionally I believed I had prepared, but I had only conceptualized what was ahead of me; life and its experiences would show me reality quickly.

Insisting that I stay rather than do what I deemed best, Mom and my stepdad tried to talk me out of

112

joining the Marines. Given they had made choices that shaped their destiny, I wanted mine to go in an entirely different direction, even though it was still the unknown. 9/11 validated and justified my decision to join the Marine Corps and make a difference by protecting our country. Defending the freedoms we are privileged to have was a greater cause than myself. And, doing so would help me become the polar opposite of my father. At that age, I resented everything about him. I was a young man who didn't understand how my father could have two children and not see us for more than a decade, but that became my motivation to do better.

In my senior year, I took a class taught by Mr. Reimer. He gave us an assignment to study information about specific companies in the stock section of the Columbus Dispatch and select companies for our portfolio. My grandparents always had the Columbus Dispatch, so I knew exactly where to go. We were responsible for tracking prices and picking high-performing stocks. In addition, we learned about P/E ratios, dividends, and how to review a company's cash flow-to-debt ratio.

Though that was the first time I realized what a stock was and what investments were, I really enjoyed it. I didn't know they existed before then, and it ignited my desire to learn more. I didn't want to be someone who couldn't provide for his family. Watching my parents work to barely provide for us wasn't my path.

The Delayed Entry Program means you get to enlist in the military at the age of 17, but you have to leave the program within 12 months. The benefit is that you get to train with everyone else and prepare for the military. The date of my year-long conclusion in the program happened to fall on the same date as my high school graduation. While all my friends were planning their Spring Break trips to Myrtle Beach, I was mentally preparing for what I assumed would be thirteen weeks of pure hell.

I received my diploma, had a small family cookout at my grandparents' house, and was off to boot camp the same night. Before leaving, my stepdad pulled me aside and talked to me like a man. Keith looked me in the eyes and said he was very proud of me. That was the only time he made me feel that I had accomplished something.

## JOHNN(Y)

The Marine Corps put me in a hotel in Columbus until the following evening. Then I flew out of Columbus Metro Airport to the Marine Corps Recruit Depot on Parris Island in South Carolina. It was the first time I'd ever been on an airplane, and I didn't know it was possible to be nervous, scared, and excited simultaneously. Intently watching the news as the war in Iraq heated up in 2003, I knew I'd find my way into combat.

I didn't prepare for another path and certainly didn't think I had another option. My high school guidance counselor didn't sit down with me and help me plan my next steps after graduating. He also didn't communicate that I had a chance to excel in life. But I imagined the courage it would take to go to war would prove what I was capable of and show that I became more than anyone expected. It didn't matter because I had a bigger plan.

No one considered that I could change my family's destiny, even if that meant I would die. Needing to accomplish more, I was willing to take that chance to create a better life than I'd ever known. It wasn't just for me; it was for my future family. Changing the course would break our generational cycle. I didn't want us to be known as a bunch of hillbillies or rednecks from Kentucky with poor grammar. Curious to discover more about life and ways to serve others, I believed that being a Marine was my only way out. Those words of Herman back in the Holler rang true; my only way out was going to war.

By the time we landed, the sun had set, and the recruits boarded a bus that took us to the island. It was the first time I saw palm trees, though I could only see their silhouettes as the moon peeked through the palm leaves. The climate was different. It was wet, and I tasted salt in the thick air. Although it seemed like paradise, once we turned down the long road to Parris Island, I knew it was anything but. As soon as we pulled up to the depot, the angry berating from drill instructors began. They sprinted onto the bus like rabid dogs, yelling, spitting, and head-butting us with their olive drab drill instructor cover.

We couldn't scramble off the bus fast enough to stand on the yellow footprints outside the receiving building, get our instructions, and learn our new way of life. They let us know we were maggots. Scum of the earth. Nothing more than a worthless piece of shit. What the United States shit out, and we were all that was left to defend it. Our leadership claimed we'd never become anything; therefore, dying on the battlefield was our contribution to giving back to the greatest nation in the world. I thought I had done everything possible to avoid feeling that way about my life, but somehow a part of me took stock of what he said, believing he was right.

The caveat to all the madness was that they promised we would eventually become U.S. Marines—and that's all I cared about. We were stripped of all our personal possessions and had our heads shaved at a speed that seemed impossible for a haircut. And when I looked in the mirror, hell, the haircut was punishment. The barber ran the clippers across my head so swiftly that my scalp bled.

Learning the rules and regulations of the Uniform Code of Military Justice was just an introduction. For the next three to four days, I didn't sleep. I doubt any of us did. But it didn't take long to discover that I could sleep standing. Then, as if we were cut off from our past life, the drill instructor advised us to make the call to tell our parents we arrived safely and nothing more because we wouldn't see or speak with them for 13 weeks. And once we did, our new life began. The Johnny they knew and the one I thought I knew would no longer exist. The Marines would tear us down and rebuild our psyches as needed. They wanted us ready.

We have the propensity to build things up in our minds and make them something they're not. I looked around boot camp thinking, *I got here by training my ass off for a year straight. If you want to yell, fine. My stepdad yelled at me often.*

Being in the Delayed Entry Program served as my commitment to the Marines, helping me maintain discipline, personal preparation, and training. Before I entered boot camp, I was promoted to Private First Class. I was surprised by some of the recruits and how out of shape they were; many lacked mental fortitude. The majority of the recruits were mentally weak, often crying, yelling they couldn't do something or wanting to quit. A lot of the platoon started looking to me for encouragement and motivation to help them keep moving forward, as I never quit and worked to create unity.

The drill instructors (DIs) noticed I was emerging as a leader, so they made me a Squad Leader out of approximately 90 guys in our platoon. Besides some of the other squad leaders, I didn't make close friends in boot camp. However, we were trained not to, as the Marines were built upon a chain of command. If we were friends with those lower in command, they might not take orders when needed.

Earning my dress blues in boot camp for being a squad leader was an accomplishment. I didn't know I'd see progress so soon, but developing those characteristics proved fruitful. Although a hunting rifle and an M-16A1 rifle were completely different, once we started shooting at the range, my natural skillset came together, earning the respect of the DI when he recognized that I'd quickly become an expert marksman. Hunting squirrels and groundhogs paid off.

South Carolina from June through September was brutally hot and what made it worse was that Parris Island had sand fleas. If the heat exceeded a specific temperature, we had "black flag" days where we didn't train outside, but we hated that, too. Every rack and footlocker were flipped, and our belongings dumped into large piles by the drill instructors, forcing us to clean everything up, Mach speed.

We had an Indy 500 race where the DIs poured cleaning chemicals on the floor and made us race each other by cleaning up the bleach with our shirts. Then, we had to bear crawl for hours pushing the water and bleach with our shirts while making race car noises as we scrubbed in a large circle. Afterward, reluctantly, we put our shirts back on, and proceeded to work out for a few more hours despite our noses running and eyes burning from the pungent stench of bleach. The DIs explained they were training us for the gas chamber.

When someone did something wrong or the platoon messed up, they took us outside to the sand pit for punishment. When those sand fleas jumped inside our uniforms and bit us, it hurt and itched like hell, making it challenging to stay focused. That heat, combined with the sand fleas, became my first experience with mental exhaustion. However, I quickly figured out that the proper mindset and attitude would allow me to persevere. I used the sand pit training as a way to understand what I might face in Iraq. I trained in the rain and heat, which helped me adopt a stronger

120

mindset that pushed negative elements such as the weather or someone screaming at me out of my mind. Adapting to the most undesirable conditions allowed me to recalibrate my mindset in preparation to focus on the objective.

It didn't take long before I learned that everything we did in boot camp, from standing in line, marching, chain of command, how we cleaned our rifles, and anything else we did, was a lesson. The Marine Corps looks at boot camp as a way to take who we were and destroy it mentally and physically. Through that process, they mold us into the Marine Corps, recreating our mindset and who we are as a person.

Integrity, commitment, and discipline are fundamental Marine Corps values, and it's instilled through a three-step process. First, they tear the old part of us away. Next, they instill Marine Corps values and traits in us. Then, after arduous training and being put in incredibly adverse situations, we come out of the fire as Marines—proving what we've learned and are capable of. The Marine Corps ethos is honor, courage, and commitment. We live and fight by those values, as there's nothing more important than the character of a Marine.

A few months prior to boot camp, I watched a Marine Corps recruitment commercial where a young man fought a dragon with a sword in a fiery hell. After defeating the dragon on top of a mountain, he transformed into a Marine wearing his full-dress blue uniform. My entire life was spent fighting dragons. I wanted nothing more than to be a Marine, to prove I could set and exceed expectations for my life. Unfavorable history would no longer dictate my future.

Everything we did emphasized teamwork, which would be critical to our survival. They taught us the history of the Marine Corps and martial arts, but the most challenging aspect was swimming. The pool was deep and extremely loud with an echo, and drill instructors were running around yelling and diving in to save guys. It was a chaotic place, making it difficult to calm your mind. As a kid, I had access to the city pool at Ted Lewis Park in Circleville. I never had any issues with swimming until they prepared us to do it the Marine Corps way.

There were two platforms to jump off. Qualifying meant doing it in full combat gear, wearing our "cammies" (the standard Marine uniform worn during training and overseas), boots, Kevlar helmet, a 30- to 40-pound backpack, and rifle. We had to jump in and tread water for a long time. The DIs taught us some strategies and how to use our uniform to help us, but the key to all of them was to refrain from panicking. Water adds fear to whatever we're doing.

Adding chaos while in the water creates heightened fear. The DI helped us understand that if we could calm our fears and remain in a mindset of clarity without panicking, we'd start to make rational decisions instead of irrational ones. The harder we fought the water, the easier it was to drown. If we remained calm and allowed our bodies to move through the water without being too chaotic, we proceeded with clarity and composure to tread water lightly. I found this to be applicable in life. I had to swim distances that I'd never done before, and I had to do it carrying other Marines. Too often, we waste time fighting opinions, circumstances, outcomes, and ourselves. However, if we allow the flow of life to navigate our minds through a sense of calmness and clarity, we can avoid the chaos this world produces.

When Marines go to boot camp at Parris Island, we usually go to the School of Infantry in North Carolina at Camp Lejeune. I wanted to be in the Marine Corps Infantry, 0311. The entire Marine Corps is built around the Marine Corps Infantry. Every role outside the infantry is there to support the only Military Occupational Specialties (MOS) that matter: 0311. To make it to a Scout Sniper Platoon like Carlos Hathcock or potentially Force Recon, I'd have to move up through the Infantry first.

However, halfway through boot camp, one of my DIs pulled me aside. He told me they were changing my Military Occupational Specialties (MOSs) because my General Technical score (GT) was too high to be in the infantry, and this move was best for the Marine Corps and me. They needed Land Assault Vehicle (LAV) drivers. I'd never heard of it. One of the recruits explained what they looked like, and I concluded it was a coffin on wheels. The roof hatches even opened like a coffin.

## JOHNN(Y)

I hated the idea of becoming a LAV driver. I was better on my feet and more confident with my rifle and tactical capabilities against the enemy than stuck in a six-wheeled coffin. Nevertheless, for my country, I'd do whatever the Marine Corps required of me. I was still required to go through the School of Infantry, but the only LAV school was in California. So, after boot camp, I returned home and spent a week with my family; then, with my orders in hand, I headed to Camp Pendleton for the next stage of my journey.

# SAND(FLEAS)

## FORGE • AHEAD

**LYING FACE-DOWN IN** *the sand, breathing the stifling air while sand fleas jumped all over me, biting, is an experience that every Marine who trains on Parris Island understands. The flea is an amazing creature, and I believe we could learn much from it. Sand fleas can jump up to 15 inches, vertically 150 times their own height. However, if you were to place sand fleas inside a bucket, they would only be able to jump the height of the bucket. This is because the lid restricts their ability. If you conditioned the sand fleas to only know the distance to the lid and removed it, the sand fleas would never jump higher than the lid allowed, even with the top removed.*

*For a substantial part of my existence, I was ensnared within the confines of the surroundings allotted to me. The viewpoints and judgments of others were imposed upon me, gradually merging with my own and affecting my perspectives. I had forged a metaphorical lid that capped* my aspirations, letting me soar only to a certain height of my family's accomplishments, which were few.

My enlistment into the Marine Corps signified the initial stride towards dismantling this ceiling and changing the course of my family legacy. However, I faced a formidable challenge—to see if I could propel myself a 150 times higher, considering my personal growth, core values, and the person I aspired to be. I was primed to tackle this challenge, but the lid had to be removed first. Like sand fleas, we can achieve great feats and surmount hurdles regardless of feeling diminutive or inconsequential.

When looking back on my environment and upbringing, here are a few ideas that I recognized helped change my trajectory:

- **CHALLENGE YOUR ASSUMPTIONS**: Question the validity of beliefs that are inherited from your upbringing or surroundings. Consider alternative perspectives without being disrespectful to those who may believe something different.

- **CHANGE YOUR LENS**: Take some time to reflect on how your upbringing and surroundings have influenced your beliefs, values, and behaviors.

Recognize any limiting beliefs or patterns that may be holding you back.

- **SET PERSONAL GOALS**: Define your aspirations and ambitions. Set specific, achievable goals that align with your values and desires, and take proactive steps to pursue them. For me, becoming a Marine was the only personal goal I focused on.

- **SEEK NEW EXPERIENCES**: Step outside of your comfort zone and expose yourself to new environments, cultures, and experiences. Travel and engage in hobbies to expand your horizons and challenge your preconceptions.

- **CONTINUOUS LEARNING**: Commit to a lifelong learning and personal development strategy. Stay curious, remain open to new ideas, and actively seek opportunities for self-improvement through education, skill-building, and self-reflection.

Like sand fleas, we can achieve great feats and surmount hurdles, regardless of feeling diminutive or inconsequential. Never stop learning, growing, and experiencing new heights.

Mr. Reimer, thank you.

# JOHNN(Y)

# SAND(FLEAS)

# gold(teeth)

## JOHNN(IE)

---

**MY KNEES WERE CAUSING** more pain than I wanted to admit. Coach Daniels ensured I was in the best shape possible, not necessarily for him or the team, but for me. He hooked me up with a physical therapist that I'd visit when I had a free period or after school. Although my knees never felt the same, I pushed through the pain. For the most part, I was okay, but they'd start bothering me at different points. During one game, we had a delay due to lightning, and my knees felt terrible. I was out there limping like something I'd never experienced. I had to believe that, in time, the pain would dissipate, and things would get back to normal because I didn't know how to stop.

For training, we transitioned from powerlifting to CrossFit lifting. The movements were different. We did more hang cleans, push-ups, power cleans, and running between workouts. I was used to running and lifting, which made the transition smooth, and it was nice to learn something different. Everybody wanted to be Chad Johnson because he personified a Florida dude. He was all the way Florida! Big personality, gold teeth— just different. And the way he acted and played the game was on another level.

He was a beast! Chad said, "They don't pay me for my game, baby. They pay me for my feet! Pay attention," and I did. I stayed hungry the following year. I was always in the weight room trying to get super big, and my work ethic continued to evolve. I wanted to take things to the next level. When scholarships started coming in, it only encouraged me to work harder and get more. I didn't want to be a good player; I wanted to be the best player in the country.

While initially I was a little knucklehead, Coach Daniels and football provided a better view of my potential.

## JOHNN(IE)

In the 2012-2013 season, we reached the point that colleges were contacting us directly on social media. Most of them called with offers, and their coaches came to see me. Bins of college and scholarship letters came in for my teammates and me. It felt crazy working for something my whole life and seeing it finally pay off. For a lot of people coming out of the hood, athletics is the way. We didn't believe we were good enough to get an academic scholarship, so we gave whatever sport we played everything we had. It was a dope experience going into the coach's office to read the letters.

The first scholarship offer I received came from the Miami Hurricanes. Being from southeast Florida, Miami was the desired destination. The University of Miami is the alma mater of Devin Hester and Ray Lewis, two of the players I most admired. At first I was super excited about Miami, but in reality I'd grown up a University of Florida fan. Had I missed their game on Saturday, I would watch the rerun on Sunday. So, when I got an offer from the University of Florida Gators, I was excited because they were my dream school. I thought it was a wrap! All-American Matt Elam was from my neck of the woods. Playing at William T. Dwyer High School before me, to us, he was a football legend. But I did my due diligence and read every offer.

My senior year, Alabama had already extended my third offer, yet Coach Saban still took the time to visit so we could discuss their offer in person. I was off campus getting rehab for my knees. He traveled with his tight-end coach, who recruited in our area, and I thought he was cool. We talked about football and how he pictured me as part of his team. Coach Saban seemed like a man of few words, but the conversation was good.

After Miami, Florida, and Alabama came the Ohio State University. Head coach Urban Meyer, arguably one of the best college coaches of all time, sat on our couch with Zach Smith, position coach and recruiter of my area, and told Mama and me what they had to offer and how they saw me fitting into their program. A follow-up visit to Ohio State convinced me I belonged there. They seemed more focused on a bigger life picture than football, just like Coach Daniels.

Coach Meyer talked in a way that none of the other college coaches did, causing me to believe in the atmosphere I was already loving by being on campus. I was seeing people of my same skin color coming from similar backgrounds, yet they were bankers or executives in high-ranking companies doing well with their lives. It made me feel that when football eventually ended, I'd be ready for the real world. I called Mama from the practice field that Sunday, explaining that Ohio State felt like home.

"I'm going to commit here."

She sighed thoughtfully, advising, "Let's just wait a little bit."

After putting all the offers on the table to assess them, I thought about what was best for me. Admittedly, I worried about how Mama would do without me if I left, especially not being able to come to every game or laugh together in the way that only we did. The biggest thing was not having her food because nothing compared. But I wanted to get away and figure out life on my own. If I went to Miami, I couldn't do that because I was only an hour away. I needed to be a man and stand on my own two feet. I was ready to grow up and see more of the world, more than I was used to. I believed it was time.

Ranked as one of the top receivers in the state and one of the best in the country, I was confident and didn't have any doubts about my path. We had a commitment party with family, friends, and coaches so I could make my announcement. Oddly, knowing I wasn't ready to make a decision that night, I announced to everyone in attendance, "Thank you all for coming, but I'm not going to commit tonight."

Weeks later, we won the state championship my senior year at Dwyer. I waited until the state championship game, where we planned a press conference for my announcement. Pops came, too, but he pulled into the parking lot and, feeling he wouldn't be accepted among the family, he didn't come out of the car. I walked out on the field wearing an Ohio State ball cap while the Miami coach sat in the stands. I had to be happy wherever I ended up, and Mama was all the way down with my choice: Ohio State.

When I told Coach Daniels I wanted to graduate early to leave for college sooner, he told me how to do it successfully. I went to work to make it happen. After intense training, I studied, attended night school with a few teammates, and prepared for the next level of my journey. Laser-focused on football—that fire burned inside me, and I threw out anything that may have been construed as a distraction. Voted homecoming king, I decided not to participate, and I didn't go to prom either. I was set on protecting my energy and focus. I knew where I wanted to be and nothing else mattered.

# FORGE • AHEAD

**OCHO CINCO WAS AN** icon to us Florida players. He was who we aspired to be as Wide Receivers, from the on-field persona to the off-field fit. As kids playing the game, we wanted to have the attention and skill set that Chad brought to the league. Oftentimes we create a persona without realizing the effect it may have on others. Those who are influencers, NFL players, politicians and corporate leaders need to carry themselves in a way to inspire others to be better. But most importantly, create a healthy mindset that others can follow.

Today there are many young athletes who look for role models and sometimes find the wrong people to emulate. When I was younger, I might have not realized the importance of the following values or looked for them within a role model. If you're an athlete or even the parent of an athlete, here are a few positive values that I would seek in a role model:

- **POSITIVE ATTITUDE**: *Find a role model who maintains a positive attitude and mindset even through adversity. Witnessing a player shove or yell at a coach during times of adversity and loss may not be a great role model.*

- **HUMILITY**: *Look for a role model who demonstrates humility and grace, both in victory and defeat. These athletes remain grounded, show respect for their opponents, and recognize the contributions of others to their success.*

- **EMPATHY**: *Seek out a role model who shows empathy and compassion toward others. These athletes use their platform to advocate for causes they believe in, support their teammates and fellow athletes, and give back to their communities.*

- **INTEGRITY**: *Find those who exemplify integrity and ethical behavior. As the saying goes, "integrity is doing what is right when no one is looking." Someone who shows strong character not just in front of the camera, but more importantly behind it.*

- **LEADERSHIP**: *Seek a role model who exhibits strong leadership qualities on and off the field. These athletes inspire and motivate others, lead by*

139

example, and use their influence to empower and uplift those around them.

By identifying and learning from role models who embody these values, athletes can cultivate a healthy mindset that supports their growth, resilience, and success both in sports and in life.

Coach Meyer, thank you.

# stab(bed)

## JOHNN(Y)

---

I MET A LOT of recruits at Camp Pendleton, including my best friend, Jon Collins. We were bunkmates. He was on the top bunk, and I was on the bottom. At the School of Infantry, we lined up alphabetically for almost everything, so Jon and I were always in proximity to each other. Davidson was the guy between us, and the three of us became best friends.

Jon and I hung out every weekend, and Davidson often came along. Davidson and I were also in boot camp, so it was great to have a familiar face join me at the School of Infantry. Our guide to our class was Cody Alford, who seemed to be at the School of Infantry for a while and was the only Lance Corporal in the class. I never understood how he was promoted to Lance Corporal, but it was easy to see Cody would go far in the Marine Corps. He led by example while holding those around him accountable, which was a formidable trait.

After being in High-Intensity Tactical Training all week, trying to recalibrate for a moment, Jon added humor to everything—and we laughed a lot. Jon and I took a trip on the Amtrack to downtown San Diego and found a tattoo parlor. We sat in chairs next to each other and got our first tattoos, commemorating the Marine Corps and our brotherhood. Jon tattooed the traditional eagle, globe, and anchor. I took a different approach by creating a tattoo of the letters USMC in chrome. It reflected everything around me with a tribal band to represent the tradition and flames above with the word "warrior" within, signifying that I had become a warrior within for the Corps. Unknowingly, Jon made this part of my journey the best. I learned how to find humor in adversity from Jon.

While we were held to the highest standards, mistakes were still made and they weren't quickly forgotten. A group of us were at the range training on shooting maneuvers and were scheduled to stay there to continue with a night fire exercise. One of the Butter Bar lieutenants was overseeing the exercise. We called the new lieutenants "Butter Bar" because of their one gold bar insignia that resembled the Country Crock butter my grandmother often left out in a small dish. Most of the time, they were right out of college and assumed they knew everything about war, leadership, and combat tactics; however, I found this was rarely the case.

In error, someone told the platoon sergeant, instead of the lieutenant, not to light off parachute flares because of the fire warning. That night, the conditions were dry with high winds, and someone lit up a parachute flare without knowing or heeding the warning. The wind took that parachute flare back behind the mountains, and we watched it trail off. About 30 minutes later, there was a wide glow on the backside of the mountain. It didn't take long before we discovered it wasn't a glow. The whole mountain had caught fire!

That guy got in trouble, but the lesson about teamwork and communication that we were taught in boot camp became clearer. At the same time, we started to realize there were a lot of miscommunications and, sometimes, a need for common sense. In war, there is no room for error. Excellent communication and common sense are equally needed, and a lack thereof can lead to death.

I graduated from the School of Infantry in the top ten percent of the class. I didn't graduate as a squad leader, but I had friends who did, and they did a great job. The barracks were U-shaped, with a little courtyard and a concrete pad in the middle, and on graduation day, they set us up outside and announced where we were going. I knew I was sent to California to attend LAV school. Given it didn't start for six months, the word was that I'd go home to Ohio and help the recruiter, then return and continue with LAV training. I was still upset about missing my opportunity to join the infantry, and along with Jon and Davidson, I voiced my desire to our platoon sergeant.

"The Marine Corps will tell you where they need you," he always replied. They started sprouting orders beginning with A names and ran through the list. They got to Jon.

"2/4, 2nd Battalion, 4th Marines, at Camp
Pendleton."

They got to Davidson and announced, "Davidson,
2/4," the same unit as Jon. So, when he called my name,
I expected him to say LAV school, as agreed.

"Dawson, 3rd Battalion, 7th Marines, Twentynine
Palms." Then he laughed and said, "Congratulations,
Dawson, you're back in the Infantry." I thought it was
great because it sounded like a vacation, but then I
wondered, where in the heck is Twentynine Palms?
Then, I found out it was the Marine Corps Air Ground
Combat Center in Twentynine Palms, California.

It's not often that we meet people who genuinely
impact us. Although our paths may not have intersected
for the duration of my military career, if I wasn't sent to
LAV school, I wanted to go with Jon and Davidson. They
both looked up to me as a leader, and I wanted to lead
them into combat, knowing I would die for them. But I
was incredibly disappointed that they sent me to 3/7.
Only one other guy, Diffley, received orders for 3/7 in
Twentynine Palms.

I thought we'd go to the airport and take a flight to
Twentynine Palms, but instead we boarded a big charter

bus from San Diego and made a five-hour ride up north. Once we got into the high desert toward Joshua Tree, there was nothing but darkness, the type I'd never known. I knew the Appalachian Mountains became dark, but the desert had reached its purest form. I couldn't see anything.

It was 1:00 a.m. when Diffley and I got to the duty station. When we checked in with the officer, he looked at us flatly and said, "I don't know why you guys are here. We're not supposed to be getting anyone tonight."

We looked at each other and walked back outside. I stood there staring into the abyss, trying to determine why the entire base smelled like shit, while the officer on duty made a call to figure out what to do with us. He was on the phone for the longest time before coming out to inform us, "Hey, I've got good and bad news. The good news is you get to stay. The bad news is you're going to 2/7, and they leave for Iraq in a few weeks."

It was December 2003. I'd been out of high school for barely six months before calling Mom to tell her I had to go to Iraq in a couple of weeks. It was already a difficult conversation, and then I heard her cry.

146

Reassuringly, I explained, "This is why I joined the Marine Corps and what I signed up to do. Mom, I have the most elite military training in the world, and we're going to be just fine. No one on the planet can defeat us."

---

PREPARING FOR IRAQ, I checked into the armory and got an armory card to retrieve my weapons. When they gave me my supplies, they were all new. When the team leaders, Lance Corporal Delvalle and Lance Corporal Fry, saw my weapons, they glanced at each other as if I wasn't supposed to have them. Lance Corporal Delvalle asked, "How did you get a new Ka-Bar, and we have these old ones, Boot?"

Being called a Boot wasn't a compliment. Anyone considered a junior was called a "boot." And when someone in a higher rank asked a question, it was always direct and intimidating. Boots knew to think before replying and to be very respectful in the process, almost like boot camp. My grandfather taught me to hand someone a knife by the handle first, and when I pulled my Ka-Bar out of its sleeve, Delvalle's back was to me—big mistake! As he rotated, his elbow hit the end of the knife. Stabbing me through the meaty part of my thumb, it sliced straight through my hand. It happened so fast that I wasn't sure how to react.

To my unit, it appeared that I had stabbed myself in the first five minutes of being there! Embarrassed and afraid to say anything, I slipped my hand into my pocket. I could feel my entire hand becoming warm, blood pouring into my pocket and filling to the point of dripping.

When Lance Corporal Delvalle saw the blood flowing down my pant leg onto the floor, he snapped. "What? Are you on your period, Boot!?"

I couldn't say, "You stabbed me," so I replied, "No, Lance Corporal!"

"Go to the corpsman station, dumbass!" he shouted angrily.

I could only imagine how the Marines in my platoon felt after hearing I stabbed myself with my Ka-Bar. I felt demoralized within the first 15 minutes of meeting the leaders of my platoon. I knew I would have to impress them after that incident somehow. The corpsman, Doc

Browning, was preparing to work on my hand, and when he struggled to get the hook in, he bent the needle straight. Then, he tried again and bent that suturing needle.

"I've got to get another," he casually confessed, walking away. On his third attempt, his face was covered in perspiration and his hand trembled when he added additional force to penetrate my skin. The skin ripped through the other side of the meaty part of my thumb, and when blood squirted on my face everything turned black.

I don't know how long it took before I came to, but when my eyes fluttered open, he asked, "Why'd you pass out?"

"You stabbed me with a needle. Where in the hell did you learn to stitch someone?"

"You're my first one," he replied, proudly.

With light laughter, I agreed, "Oh, that makes perfect sense."

"Well, you can't go to the field with your hand like this. It pierced clean through to the bone."

The medical command didn't want me to go to the field. We were out there doing a work-up before departing for Iraq. They were concerned the week-long field exercises could infect my hand, causing more damage from working in the sand. Still, I demanded they allow me to go after vehemently explaining Iraq was precisely why I needed to be with my platoon.

"Just give me a few stitches and some gauze and send me to the field," I insisted.

Surprisingly, they complied. Doc wrapped my hand and gave me enough gauze for the week, making it clear that I had to check in with him daily to have it cleaned.

The senior guys took me under their wings and taught me the ropes of the fleet and how to become a hard-charging infantryman. They were grooming me to become the platoon's Radio Operator (RO), which I deemed a compliment.

Joining 2/7, I was starting over again because the new guys always got hazed. They had sleepovers where they'd make us buy popcorn, bring a blanket, and watch *Full Metal Jacket* or some other motivational military movie. We'd work out for hours or until we puked, then, creating chaos and causing amusement, they'd make us fight and wrestle. The Boots of 1st platoon would fight the other platoons, and we'd capture each other's platoon flags and then see how long we could fight off their platoon.

Echo Company 1st Platoon, we called ourselves the Pirates of the Palms, proudly displaying a black pirate flag with two crossed bones and a skull. We considered ourselves the best platoon, but so did every platoon— each had its own culture. The flag had been a long tradition, passed down since Vietnam. We had a Ka-Bar that was passed down, too. Delvalle gave me the Ka-Bar, also known as the Marine Corps bayonet, which was passed down to him once he left the Marine Corps. It was an honor to receive the Ka-Bar, and ironic considering he stabbed me with one!

Following our work-up in the field and spending more time with the platoon, I was ready to go to Iraq and confident to head into war. At 18, I was trained by the best military in the world, who taught me to operate without fear. I had prepared for eight months, and it was time to test everything. Though I felt a sense of excitement, the unknown was something I had yet to face.

A few days later, the buses were lined up, and spouses and families assembled to give us a big send-off. Since no one was there to see me off, I moved aside, and checked my gear, mentally pulling it together. Although everyone enlisted, not everyone was ready or willing to serve. On the way to the buses, one of the guys put on his Kevlar and flak jacket, opened the door, and jumped out! He tried to injure himself so he wouldn't be sent to Iraq. When he got to the buses, the entire unit heard his wife cussing him out, spewing obscenities that even Marines shouldn't hear. The military police handcuffed and arrested him.

The three-story commercial liner on that 17-hour flight was the biggest plane I'd ever been on. We stopped in Germany, where we landed to an armed German military escorting us across the tarmac. They had everything blocked off, preventing German civilians from knowing we were there. Our final stop was Kuwait, and we traveled with our M16 rifles and packs. On the flight, the staff were the friendliest and most sincere people, expressing their gratitude for what we were about to do. But sadness or trepidation rested in their eyes as if understood and unspoken that there were Marines on the flight who would never return home.

# JOHNN(Y)

Eventually, the Marine they arrested was sent to Iraq to run our internet. They'd given him a fake wooden Ka-Bar to carry around for the longest time before assigning him a rifle, and when he got his rifle, everyone watched him very closely—no one trusted him.

# STAB(BED)

## FORGE • AHEAD

**OFTEN, WE FACE CIRCUMSTANCES** *in which we have created a premeditated outcome. For me, the initial start of my Marine Corps journey wasn't anything that I would have imagined. From going to the School of Infantry in California, to being told I was switching my MOS, to not switching my MOS, to suddenly leaving for Iraq almost immediately, all the while being stabbed by my own team leader the first day in the fleet! Without the proper mindset, I could have allowed all these early adversities to affect my mindset and cause me a state of anxiety.*

*Facing adversities can potentially cause a lot of anxiety and be challenging, but it can also be a transformative experience if you allow it. When I was at the Corpsman station receiving stitches, I knew I needed to change my mindset to overcome this adversity and prove to my unit I could contribute and become a leader. Here are a few lessons I feel could help overcome any adversity that you may be facing:*

- **REFRAME ADVERSITIES AS OPPORTUNITIES:** Instead of viewing adversity as insurmountable obstacles, see them as an opportunity for growth and learning. Embrace challenges as a chance to develop resilience, problem-solving skills, and inner strength. (See Psalm 50:15)

- **FOCUS ON WHAT YOU CAN CONTROL:** Do not dwell on things beyond your control; instead, focus your energy on the aspects of the situation that you can influence. (See Psalm 56:3)

- **ACCEPT THE CHALLENGE:** Accept that adversity is a natural part of life, and that experiencing discomfort is inevitable at times. Recognize that it is okay to feel anxious or overwhelmed, but also acknowledge that you have the ability to navigate those emotions and forge a stronger mindset. (See Psalm 23:4)

- **STAY PRESENT:** Practice mindfulness and stay grounded in your faith. Do not dwell on past regrets or future worries. (See Jeremiah 29:11)

- **CELEBRATE PROGRESS:** Acknowledge and celebrate small victories and progress, no matter how incremental. Recognize your resilience and

155

perseverance in the face of adversity and use these moments as fuel to forge ahead. (See 1 Corinthians 15:57)

Adjusting your mindset to see adversity as an opportunity can not only relieve mental health stress, but also increase your overall health, mindset, and attitude.

Delvalle, thank you.

# JOHNN(Y)

# black(stripes)

## JOHNN(IE)

**I ENTERED OHIO STATE** confident and ready for this part of my journey. The team was coming off a loss in the Orange Bowl, so they were focused on an upcoming undefeated season and winning the national championship. We worked hard in high school, but Ohio State had a different pace, focus, and discipline. Physical training was a big adjustment because their workouts were unlike anything I'd ever done. Coach Mickey Marotti, our strength and conditioning coach, kicked our butts in sports performance. All-encompassing, we were working at a whole new level just to be competitive and get playing time. Not everyone could go in and play right away. There were a lot of superstars on our team.

The coaches were relentless with early workouts, mat drills, and the Valentine's Day massacre workout, which was designed to test your limits and see what you've really got inside of you. Sweat everywhere. Grown men screaming out from pain as they pushed even harder than what seemed physically possible. Blood. Vomit. Men dropping to the ground in pure exhaustion. Our first mat drills consisted of wrestling with bags and tires, crazy jumps, twists, and turns. It was different and challenging, but I could do it because I had mental fortitude; I just had to block out everything else, including my knee pain.

When I saw that Raekwon "Kwon" McMillan committed to Ohio State University on Dec 16, 2013, I tweeted, *I see you, boy!* And Raekwon replied, *You next, my boy!* I came early to college in January with Kwon. We were roommates. Trying to navigate where to find a barber who could cut and keep me fresh, I told Kwon I needed a haircut. I had to find a good barber. Kwon said, "No, let's not. Let's look rough." So, taking his advice, I let my hair grow out, and Kwon was right, we looked hard, but our work ethic was always harder.

Urban Meyer had this thing he called "black stripes" on our helmets for incoming freshmen. Wearing a black stripe signifies that you are not yet a part of the team. You are an outsider. You lack the work ethic, commitment, passion, and teamwork required to be a Buckeye. It had an unspoken message that was clear to see, and everyone knew they would have to work harder than ever to prove they could be a Buckeye. Once that stripe was removed, we knew we were part of the brotherhood—a family. We were coming together to create a cohesive whole and an unstoppable force. What I didn't expect was that I would become part of a team that cared not only about my athletic ability, but more importantly—me.

Kwon was the first dude to ever get his black stripe off in spring ball. He set a good example for the rest of us, and I wanted to be like him. I didn't realize it at the time, but Kwon pushed me more than I ever knew. He was thorough with his homework, teamwork, and work ethic, but we still had time to laugh every day. Just

Kwon being who Kwon was made life there more enjoyable.

The harder I worked physically proved to put more stress on my knee injuries, intensifying the pain. Since I managed to push through in high school, I did everything possible to mentally do the same at Ohio State. I continued doing workouts at the highest level, especially since every coach's eye was on the new recruits because they already knew what the older guys could do.

Six of us came in early that season, and initially, they had us working out on our own, learning the ropes before we were integrated. That's when I discovered that Ohio State's brotherhood was the realest. The older guys looked out for us and made our adjustment seamless. Coming from the hood, I always had older cats who did the same, which was the feeling Curtis Grant gave me. He took us under his wings, on and off the field, and ensured we were invited to everything. He invited us to BBQs and things the more senior teammates organized, intentionally connecting us freshman to the more seasoned guys.

They taught us lessons in respect, mentorship, work ethic, and what brotherhood is while helping us navigate this part of the journey. Sitting in one of our many meetings, I looked around realizing that one day, we would be the "old heads," and there would be younger guys coming in to play over us. What my new teammates demonstrated allowed me to develop into the leader I wanted to be at Ohio State. It was like they were passing the torch from one generation to the next; handing down the knowledge and wisdom they had acquired over the years so we could use it to be set up for success.

In high school, I knew I could play at the highest level with my injury, but it wasn't without work and making adjustments all spring to figure things out. Ohio State was on a different level. Intense. After spring ball and fall practice, I was ready to go, and we began our season. As a receiver, I had plays where I ran sweeps and everything, but I could feel the physical challenges more than ever. Even though I was hurt, I was determined to play. I'd have a really good day, but then my knees would feel like crap the next day. I wanted to be the best player I could be. I worked my tail off to play as a freshman and prove to the coaches that I was the person I was hyped up to be. I pushed through the pain, refusing to submit mentally—but physically, my body wasn't in sync.

Initially, I thought I was okay starting my first year early—I was a Buckeye, meeting new brothers, making friends, navigating an unfamiliar environment, essentially learning and adjusting to a completely different way of life. The transition was easy, and I had fun until my injured knees became the focus and an obstacle I couldn't overcome, threatening my sole goal in life of playing professional football and being the best. I played three games that season and traveled with the team for the first game. I didn't play in the second. In the third, I had a few rushes against Kent State. When the game was done, the medical staff and Coach Meyers recommended that I have surgery. I knew I needed it.

If it got me back on the field so I could play to my potential, I was all for it. However, when they did an arthroscopy on my right knee, they diagnosed me with early-onset arthritis, most likely due to joint trauma. My left knee had Patellar Tendinitis, an injury to the tendon connecting my kneecap, the patella, to my shin, caused by repetitive stress on the patellar tendon. As a medical redshirt, I attended team meetings, did workouts, and watched practices. The problem was that I was unable to contribute to our team winning the Big Ten Championship and the National Championship over #2 ranked Oregon.

After that first year, I thought I'd be fine. I was confident surgery would fix the problem. The orthopedic surgeon cleaned up my left knee, allowing me to participate cautiously in spring ball. I was full go when fall camp began.

I had adjusted to the routine of school and football, but life—or rather the loss of lives back home—was escalating. My friends and people I knew were dying, primarily due to gun violence, and that affected my mental fortitude.

During my freshman year, someone shot a kid I grew up with for being in the car with the wrong person at the wrong time. Bullets don't discriminate! Although I wasn't there, the emotional impact was the same. The violence didn't end. When I got calls at two or three in the morning, I didn't like answering the phone, knowing someone was calling to tell me that someone I cared about was dead.

Nearly every time I logged into Facebook there were messages about someone back home who was murdered or had died, including my own cousin. The guilt of being away and trying to better my life was tremendous. Somehow, I felt that things could have been different if I had been home, as though I could have saved them, even if I'd just spoken with them more often. Every time I hung up the phone from one of those calls back home, it was a reminder that the opportunity was gone.

I was at Ohio State, in a safe environment, playing football and working on my degree while my friends were dying. It gave me such guilt. But my reality was that I needed to stay out of it and get Mama and my siblings out. I didn't want to return home because the environment had the wrong elements. When that's all there is, it was easy to get sucked in and join a gang, sell drugs, or become an addict. Football was the way out, and I needed to be successful. They depended on me.

I didn't have the time or space to grieve and process each loss, and the calls continued, one after another.

Losing loved ones became my reality, and I knew it hit hard back home. With a heavy heart, I went to practice, our games, sat in class, or tried to study. It certainly wasn't healthy, but I had to suppress my emotions to focus. I was busy focusing on the future, aware that some of my friends wouldn't see theirs.

Things were starting to hit me a bit differently; I'd wake up in my dorm room and scream, "F—k!" I knew Kwon had to be sick of me screaming that one word every single morning. And finally, he said, "You do this every morning."

It felt like he was asking what was wrong or giving me a chance to talk, but I didn't say anything. I just kept waking up yelling, "F—k!" Frustration with not playing was the beginning of expressing what I was internalizing. I didn't want to do anything if it didn't relate to playing football. I didn't like soaking in ice or doing rehabilitation on my knees; if it wasn't putting me back on the field that day, I didn't want to do it. I just wanted to play.

I returned to Ohio State for spring ball without fully processing or mourning the losses of my friends and family. They affected me deeply and I couldn't do anything except cry. When Zach saw me, he pulled me aside and kept me from participating. If I didn't know it yet, I learned then that the coaching staff's compassion was genuine. As long as they were aware something was going on with us or we told them, they did whatever they could to help.

I never had any fear so constantly on my mind until the thought of not making it to the NFL came into play. Of course, I knew what I had ahead of me once I got healthy, but I wasn't there yet. I kept having setbacks. Losing friends and people I knew was a setback. My knees were a setback. Mentally, I was being setback. When I got around my teammates, I was fine or appeared to be. However, when it came to the coaches, that was another story. I was on edge—the coaches could say anything about anything, and I'd snap, "Leave me alone!"

It was pointless to get enraged about anything, and I knew I didn't have to push issues to that level, but it wasn't intentional. When I was on campus or alone, I wasn't there all the way. No one knew it, which seems to be the theme of mental health; no one knows what anyone is internalizing and feeling. They don't know, but I sure as hell did. I didn't want to be in class or around people. Tired of being sad and agitated, to the point that every little thing bothered me, humor was my way of offsetting my feelings. At the end of the day, I'd turn on something funny, typically stand-up or YouTube. I knew I had to lock it down internally to escape the whole situation but locking it inside wasn't the best solution. I don't advise it.

That season, my knees were still nagging me—some weeks I could practice, and other weeks, they were still jacked up. Our receivers kept getting injured, and I was next in line to play. Then, on my first day back, when I finally got back on the field, I ran a slant in practice. I caught it, fell on my knee, and broke my kneecap. I was out for the rest of that season!

Instead of my normal happy self, I felt my anger rising. My fuse was shorter. It was a clear indication that I needed to talk to someone. I thought reaching beyond a family member or friend would prevent feeling awkward or judged. That meant I had to go outside my circle to the next level and find a professional who could help me out because I didn't like how I felt. I thought it was probably better to try and work out what was settling inside me. I knew I had resources, but there were so many others, even back home, who didn't. And if they did, they may not have known about it, or couldn't afford therapy. I had access.

Being an athlete—a football player—we're strong. Resilient and all that. We're built to handle anything, especially if we're playing for the best damn team in the land! But the problem was that I wasn't playing or even practicing, and I needed help coping with the rising depression and constantly being down. My life, my whole world, was football. I was trying to get into the NFL. Instead, I felt like my dreams were crumbling in front of me.

Many of us were navigating injuries, but I didn't know if anyone else felt the way I did. I thought they must have been dealing with something because playing for OSU was my path, and if I felt derailed, it had to hit some of them, too. But again, no one knew what I was struggling with mentally and emotionally, so I tried to be uplifting and encourage them while I was silently fighting depression and fear. In the Bible, Goliath held the Israelite army in fear because he seemed greater than everything else they could be combined. My injury was my Goliath, seemingly greater than any other part of me combined that I had worked so hard to make progress with over the past several years.

Anger was taking over who I was. I probably got into it with every coach, even the strength coach, and I loved that guy. I was trudging through the day wearing a fake smile, nodding, and responding. I didn't feel like talking to anyone. Winter made my mental health worse, hurling me into a deeper hole. I didn't like the person I was becoming. The anger got bad quickly without me realizing it. A day with depression meant that we had a workout planned. Why? I couldn't work out with my team and my frustration bubbled over. The coaches always told us that we had all the mental and physical support on staff we needed, so I kept that in the back of my mind, but I wasn't ready to see it.

I never had a love for school, so I couldn't blame my falling grades on depression or make any excuses. I had to get the work done because coaches and the university, as a whole, cared about our education. People try to downplay academics when it comes to athletes, but whether we play sports depends on our academics. I didn't go to every class, but I made it to tutoring and did the work because I knew what I signed up for and got it done. I got the block "O" tattooed on my left arm for a reason, not for looks. I lived and breathed being a Buckeye, which meant going the distance, and they constantly pushed me to do my best.

When I have that helmet and uniform on, I am a different person than I am without it. The work of an athlete is different, and the bar we are held to isn't the same as other students. We know it's what we signed up for, it's what we want to do and have worked our whole lives for, but the accountability is much different.

We couldn't go to a bar and get into a fight. It would be newsworthy and affect our coaching staff and athletic director. It could potentially jeopardize our ability to play if we don't adhere to the code of conduct and the values that we, as Buckeyes, have to maintain: integrity, education, people, excellence, respect, innovation, community, and tradition. There was little to no room for error.

Football is a nine to five plus overtime commitment. At the college level, there's a lot more to it, which is why I think there are numerous students and student-athletes like me who struggled with depression. Others may have anxiety or other mental health concerns, but they exist. I discovered that college was a more significant adjustment than I initially thought.

I decided to play football but at the end of the day, it's not as easy as it may look. Behind the scenes, we're fighting to keep our position while putting everything we have into football and working to balance it. The only way to completely understand what it's like for us is after having a week, or just one day like ours. I enjoyed being held to the Ohio State standard, but sometimes athletes get overwhelmed, derailed, or broken, and we need help getting back on track. We're human beings.

There came a point when the weight got too heavy, when even the smallest steps felt like slogging through quicksand. I had meetings with Coach Meyer, Coach Hartline, Coach Smith, and Adam Stewart ("Stewie") about my classes and football. When I grew tired of the emotional dips and waves, I went to Lil Stewie, all 5'5" of him, and shared some of what I was feeling. He didn't tell me anything more than anyone else had to say. But somehow, he was the right guy to get a lot off my chest. When I told him I thought I should see a mental health therapist, he didn't hesitate to point me in the right direction.

The coaches were right. Ohio State had all of the necessary resources for our physical health, but they also had support and therapists for our mental health. Access is there, but it's up to us to be honest and acknowledge what we're going through. No one can help what they can't see. People don't always recognize changes in behaviors either. And even if we don't exactly know what's wrong or what's causing the changes, it's an excellent decision to start with a therapist and find out. I wasn't embarrassed or too proud to go because I didn't want to get worse or be "stuck." A day with depression sucked!

Waking up to gray skies, it felt like the universe was confirming it: "Today's not your day." And as the days rolled on, all that I'd pushed aside, it caught up to me, heavy as a freight train. It dragged me down into a hole that seemed to have no end. Life, man, it can get to you. It hit me out of nowhere, this weird, rough patch. Sitting there, answering a battery of questions, *Am I depressed? Nah, I'm just... tired, right?* But deep down, I knew. It was like I was watching myself fall through the seasons, feeling the chill set in.

I found myself in the therapist's office, seated across from someone who was supposed to help me untangle the chaos in my head. It's not easy, you know? Where I come from, you're taught to grit your teeth and power through. As a Black man from the streets, showing cracks in your armor isn't an option—you're expected to tough it out, fix your own mess. But there I was, in a dark place, feeling lost in my own mind, struggling to navigate through the fog.

Depression—it's a beast. It scatters your thoughts, steals your joy, makes "you" a stranger to yourself. I'm the guy who's always up, always laughing, but that laughter had become a distant echo. They say it's alright to reach out, that it's okay to not be okay, regardless of whether you're a man of color or not. But still, I felt those eyes, heavy with judgment, waiting to pounce the moment I showed a hint of vulnerability.

Sometimes you need someone to lean on. It took ages to spit out the truth, to admit that the struggle to smile wasn't just a bad day—it was every day. That help, that hand reaching out, it's hard to grasp. But when you're sinking, it's not about pulling yourself up—it's about letting someone else help pull you up.

Taking that step, walking into that office, it was one of the toughest things I've done. But you gotta hit that point where you realize you can't do it all. You gotta let go of the pride, let down the guard, and just... get help.

Other athletes battle depression and anxiety, and people aren't aware of it, but they still go on the field or compete in their sport. I never saw it coming. And if we're good at going through the motions or routine and keeping it inside, people only see what they want to see. We don't play football because we're trying to provide for ourselves. Many of us have obligations to our families, children, a spouse, or something else. Often, any money we get is sent to our families. Kwon and I were so broke in college that we did everything possible to hang onto a hundred dollars for a month. The struggle is still there.

# JOHNN(IE)

## FORGE • AHEAD

**ONE OF THE TRADITIONS** *that Urban instilled within the team was the removal of the black stripe for incoming freshmen. I didn't realize it at the time, but removing that stripe included me in an environment that would provide the resources and help me overcome depression before it became darker and more challenging to manage. Many people battle depression, mental instability, and anxiety every day, and unfortunately, they don't have the tools or a "team" who checks in on them.*

*When looking at your life, are you still wearing a black stripe? Are you open to creating a community around you and joining a team, or do you continue to look at your problems as a mountain that cannot be climbed? Maybe it's time to finally remove that black stripe from your life to help you through your own mental health storm while becoming the person you were designed to be—happy.*

*Here are a few suggestions on how to create your own team:*

- **CONNECT WITH YOUR FAITH COMMUNITY**: *Reach out to your local church or other religious institution to connect with others who share your faith. Participate in community events to build relationships and you'll likely discover others who may have a similar experience.*

- **FORM SMALL GROUPS**: *Consider creating your own small group of friends and colleagues that focuses on healthy mental health conversations. These groups can provide a safe and supportive space to share experiences, struggles, and resources.*

- **PRIVATE SOCIAL MEDIA GROUPS**: *Consider joining a private social media group that relates to your circumstance and mental health state. You can then message individuals that you relate with for further support.*

- **LUNCH WITH FRIENDS**: *Decide to create a recurring lunch or coffee with a friend once a week just to discuss your mental state and have a vulnerable conversation about how you are feeling.*

- **THERAPY**: Establish a relationship with a therapist through ongoing meetings to discuss your current mental health while creating strategies to overcome any adversities you could be facing.

By actively engaging with your community and leveraging resources and support networks, you can remove your mental health black stripe for good!

Stewie, thank you.

# BLACK(STRIPES)

# flak(jacket)

## JOHNN(Y)

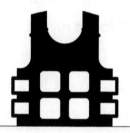

---

**WHEN WE LANDED IN** Kuwait, we were picked up by charter buses in the middle of the night and escorted across the freeway by several Kuwaiti police and U.S. military vehicles driving at high rates of speed. The bus driver even appeared uncomfortable. Curiosity ravaged our young minds when we set foot in what we called "tent city," where hundreds of large white tents filled the base. We stayed there for nearly three weeks, training, running, and discussing logistics before reaching Iraq.

We practiced giving each other IVs, placing tourniquets, and learning the 9 Line for a Medical Evacuation Request. I wore a gas mask when I ran in

120-degree heat because it made breathing harder. Some of the guys in my platoon thought I was crazy, but it worked because I knew it was preparation for what we were there to do. I intentionally trained that way to calm my breath, which taught me to focus a little deeper if I found myself in a chaotic situation.

One evening, a chaplain popped his head into our tent. "You guys are leaving in a couple of days. If you want to get baptized, come outside."

A few of the guys and I went out to find a huge tarp draped over the bed of a Humvee filled to the brim with water. The chaplain handed each of us a desert-camouflaged pocket Bible, and I began thumbing through it, trying to comprehend the contents. It was the first time I'd opened the Bible with the intent of understanding the scriptures. I'd only been to church three times in my life, and as a kid, I went to Bible study in Kentucky only a few times with Kade's kids.

I climbed in the back of the Humvee, wearing a pair of silky green shorts which were cut high and stuck to my leg in the surprisingly cold water. As the wind picked up, I felt an overwhelming sense of the Holy Spirit. I got in the water, feeling the rise of goosebumps blanketing my body. Staring at the stars, I plugged my nose as the chaplain leaned in, affirming, "You are dead to sin." He dunked my head underwater and swiftly lifted me, adding, "And alive to Christ!"

At that moment, I felt a sense of security that maybe God did have my back—and given where we were headed, I thought I'd need all the help I could get, so I started praying before every meal and at night before bed. I prayed for strength, guidance, speed, and the ability to lead my men to the best of my abilities. But, most importantly, I prayed we would all come home.

I assumed that if God put me on this path, I'd probably die by 19. Early on, I advised my team to "pray before every meal and every mission because each one could be your last." Every time we left the wire, we were staring at death while courageously doing our job and walking toward it. The assignments leadership sent us on were nothing less than pure insanity. They'd send us to look for IEDs in the middle of the night, and one of my guys, Brian, tripped on an IED. Had it gone off, all 13 of us would have blown up. I was on a tour that lasted nine months, which made death inevitable. It wasn't a lack of confidence; it was reality.

I was training to be a radio operator in Kuwait and while stationed there, they held a meritorious promotion. Each platoon had to designate one Marine to appear before command and present themselves for advancement. I was the one chosen for 1st Platoon. The command asked us tactical questions about Marine Corps history, general knowledge, and ethics. Then, depending on our answers and overall presentation, they would pick a Marine to be promoted.

I was promoted to Lance Corporal before we left Kuwait, and they made me a team leader of the designated marksmen team, the Guardian Angels. My call sign was "Ghost Rider." I was the youngest team leader in our company, causing a few senior Marines to take offense to a junior "boot" with a higher command level. But I knew I had to earn their trust, and I didn't take their perspective lightly as I was still seeking their advice and direction. The objective of our team was to find higher ground or create an element of overwatch for the platoon as we patrolled.

# JOHNN(Y)

One of the critical pieces of equipment for a Marine in combat, outside of their rifle, is the flak jacket, also known as their kit. The flak jacket can be altered to carry different pouches to hold magazines, grenades, tourniquets, night vision goggles, zip ties, and other gear required for combat. However, every flak jacket carries two ballistic proof plates, one in the front and one in the back. Though it adds a lot of additional weight, the benefit of having the plates can be the difference between life and death.

We did everything in our flak jackets: went to the bathroom, patrolled, and slept. Anytime we left our concrete walls, we wore our protection, which gave us a sense of ease when we anticipated danger. It is impossible to know precisely how many lives the flak jacket saved from gunfire or shrapnel, but I would imagine thousands of men and women went home because of this protection. The protection of the flak jacket gave us a sense of mental strength over our enemy as we knew they didn't have the same protective measures and tools.

As it turned out, we spent a lot of time in gas masks. In Iraq, part of the mission was looking for weapons of mass destruction, so we had to wear masks along with MOPP (Mission Oriented Protective Posture) suits. None of us knew what heat was until we wore full MOPP suits and gas masks. The heat was insane! The same as pitching a tent directly in front of a hot oven with a fan on the backside filled with sand. Whenever we were outside, we sweated profusely. It never stopped. Sweat was a magnet for sand and dirt, and it didn't take long for our cammies to feel like sandpaper scratching against our skin.

We flew into Al-Anbar Province on C-130s. Anyone who had been to Iraq knew this was not where we'd want to go because the likelihood of death was high. Al-Anbar Province was like the Wild West of Iraq. The Marine Corps was in control of this province, and as luck would have it, all the insurgent hotbeds were there. We traveled to Hit, Iraq, and took control of a Forward Operating Base (FOB). The FOB was previously an Iraqi Republican Guard base that sat on top of a large hill along the Euphrates River, the longest and one of the most historically significant rivers in Western Asia. One half of the team drove in, and the other half flew in. The Hit FOB had three large barracks that were two stories

184

high. They formed a U shape, and each corner had an observation post where we'd rotate guards.

We were hit with mortar fire in the first few days of staying on the FOB because the insurgents wanted to see how the new unit reacted to indirect fire. Mortar fire became much like Ohio weather because we never knew what we'd get. Whenever we heard a long whistle overhead, everyone immediately ran for cover. The first night we were mortared, everyone ran out of the barracks wearing silkies, underwear, and flak jackets with our Kevlar, as if the enemy was about to overrun our FOB and we were the only thing standing in the way.

Brian had the best outfit: barefoot, boxers with smiley faces, and a flak jacket, ready to kill anyone crossing the wire. A sight to see! We didn't know it would become a weekly routine but from then on, we couldn't go to the port-a-johns without wearing full combat gear, for fear of being mortared. I believe my biggest fear at that time was being mortared while in a port-a-john—not an ideal way to go.

One night on post, Barnard and I had water balloons from a mail supply box. We took the liberty of filling them and storing them on post—anyone going to the port-a-johns had to walk beneath us. It was about 2:00 a.m. and Corporal Durhiem, one of our Squad Leaders, started stumbling below us, most likely still half asleep. As he cleared the balcony, I threw a balloon, a direct hit on the back of Durhiem's head! He fell to his knees, screaming, "Oh God! I've been hit, I've been hit!" After hearing Barnard and I roar in laughter, he got up and cursed us out for a few minutes.

As the sun rose and the mosque played their prayers over the speakers, we started to take mortar fire. I scanned the Euphrates River looking for a plume of smoke. I found what looked to be a pick-up truck launching the mortars out of the back of the truck through the palm grooves. I immediately called for fire on the location, sending about eight mortars walking them on the location. The mortars stopped once we started firing back. That was the first time we fired mortars back at the insurgents. The other squad from our platoon patrolled down to that location, but didn't find a truck, only some damage to the houses in the surrounding area.

Staying in the same barracks as a platoon created great comradery and chemistry. The problem was there were always Marines with poor hygiene, but we handled everything internally, often duck-taping the Marines to their rack, covering them in baby powder, or hazing them until they understood their hygiene was affecting the entire platoon. In essence, we policed our own in 1st platoon.

Despite the laughs, pranks, and hazing, none of us knew—if we survived—how the remnants of this journey would affect us in the future.

---

IN 2004, WE WERE the first wave of the battle of Fallujah. "Operation Valiant Resolve" was to bring peace to Iraq's city of Fallujah by removing extremists and insurgents and finding those responsible for the March 31st ambush that killed four American military contractors. We arrived back at the Hit FOB, where several Assault Amphibious Vehicles (AAVs) were waiting for us. We didn't understand what was happening because we couldn't readily access the news or get updates on what was taking place in other parts of Iraq.

Command told us we were going into Fallujah, and we were ready. We crammed into the back of the AAV, stepping and sitting on each other. The overcrowding inside the AAV and the pungent smell of diesel combined with the heat made breathing difficult. I stood watch from the top of the hatch for the duration of the drive.

The command gave us the Rules of Engagement (ROEs) as "Recon by Fire," meaning if something looked suspicious, shoot at it. If it shoots back, kill it. And we were instructed that any military-aged male wearing all black could be shot on sight as the entire city of Fallujah was put on notice to evacuate. But the enemy didn't leave; they were everywhere, hazardously blending in. I continually found it perplexing that we would announce our advancements to the regions we would operate in, ruining the element of surprise. Those decisions were well above my pay grade and handled in hickory-decorated political offices. I was just a grunt.

We kicked in more than a thousand doors, however it seemed the insurgents were too scared to face us, so they continued to hide behind women and children, blending in with the general population. Morale started to decrease as we didn't get the fight we expected and prepared for. We started calling the mission "Operation JK"—Just Kidding. On patrol, we came across an old Toyota pickup truck. Six dead Iraqis were in the truck; two were in the front and four were in the back. Hardened blood had dripped from the insurgent's headshot wounds. Special Forces had gone through the city just days prior to our arrival. We were pretty upset that we might have missed the opportunity to finally fight the enemy rather than just patrolling, waiting to be blown up.

One night, our squad of 13 was on patrol, keeping enough distance so that if someone stepped on a landmine, it wouldn't kill everyone else. If we got into combat, we'd spread out, maintaining dispersion between us. We were at an ex-Iraqi housing area for the Republican Guard's elite troops. Observing their faces, we knew that most of them still lived there, hiding behind women and children. You could see the look through their eyes that they wanted to kill you.

The five buildings were huge, with narrow walkways between them. All the streetlights as well as lights on the building were on. Making our way across a large grassy field, heading through the courtyard, I spotted a generator at a big powerhouse. An old man with a lantern entered the building, and we heard the generator shut off, which turned off every light—leaving us in pure darkness. We had placed ourselves in the most vulnerable situation I'd ever been in, and if they set us up for an ambush, it worked. I thought we would perish in that courtyard.

Our squad quickly got out of the courtyard and took a defensive position. I didn't know if something was planned or if they shut down the generator to conserve fuel and energy, but that situation was a critical lesson. When we returned to base, we realized we had compromised our position because we had become complacent. Rather than take the faster route through the middle of an open courtyard, we should have been cautious and stayed along the buildings. Fallujah taught us that complacency can kill us. If we weren't in a heightened state of awareness all the time, we could die. It wasn't a lesson solely for my squad. It was a lesson for all of us!

# FLAK(JACKET)

## FORGE • AHEAD

**ONE OF THE MOST** *utilized pieces of gear in combat is the flak jacket; it would go anywhere that I went while facing danger. It provided a sense of security in a world that felt like death was around the corner. Sometimes in our own lives we can feel like death is around the corner. Death of a relationship, friendship, job, or even our own mental state. We always need to be mindful of the tools we have available to use on a regular basis to build our own flak jacket against the Goliath-sized thoughts that can sometimes consume our minds.*

*As we face the uphill battles that PTSD can produce, there are several resources out there to build our own "kit" of security and a sense of protection. Creating your own kit by taking proactive steps to maintain your mental health can help you prepare for and handle difficult situations more effectively. Here are a few apps that you can download to help you overcome the mental health Goliath you may be facing today:*

192

- **BIBLE APP**: *One of my most used apps, you are able to read the verse of the day, build a community, and create devotional plans tailored to how you are feeling and any adversity that you may be facing.*

- **HEADSPACE**: *This app offers guided meditation and mindfulness exercises to reduce stress, improve sleep, and increase overall well-being.*

- **PTSD COACH**: *Developed by the U.S. Department of Veterans Affairs, this app provides education about PTSD, self-assessment tools, coping strategies, and resources for finding support.*

- **SANVELLO**: *Offers tools for stress management, mood tracking, mindfulness meditation, and cognitive-behavioral therapy (CBT) techniques to support individuals with anxiety, depression, and PTSD.*

- **MOODPATH**: *Guides users through daily mood assessments, provides personalized insights, and offers resources and exercises based on cognitive-behavioral principles to support mental well-being.*

It is also essential to remember that while apps can be valuable tools for self-management and support, they are not a substitute for professional treatment. When building your own flak jacket, there is no absolute right way to construct your pouches and carry your gear; rather, by equipping yourself with tools to help you overcome your mental Goliath.

Matt, thank you.

# grid(iron)

## JOHNN(IE)

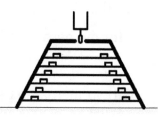

**I MET VIVIANA ONLINE** in 2015 and thought she was gorgeous. When I sent her a message, she didn't see it or even reply for a year. Eventually, we began talking and our conversations continued because the realness we shared was attractive. It wasn't until after winning the Fiesta Bowl against Notre Dame in 2016 that we finally met—in the Princess Hotel parking lot in Scottsdale, Arizona. We walked around for five hours talking and it felt like we'd known each other for years, but I learned even more about her in that long conversation.

Viviana was independent and hardworking, but her personality, the way she laughed, and how she made me feel were reminders that someone like her was rare to find. We hit it out of the park, and it didn't take long to realize that she was special. I left knowing that one day, Viv would be my wife. Despite our trust and closeness, I never told Viv what I was going through. I didn't let her see it either. It was personal. I didn't want anyone to feel sorry for me because I felt strong enough to overcome it.

Grown men aren't supposed to be weak. As men, often we suppress problems, issues, and concerns without addressing the emotions that come with them until our emotional and/or mental health becomes the problem. For an athlete, we don't have depression; we're just having a bad day. We're strong and resilient. We're the ones that encourage or inspire others. Knowing that, I kept my mental health and my feelings to myself, maintained the façade that everything was all good.

---

**BY MY THIRD YEAR,** I was fed up with the injuries and had only played a couple of games in two years. I committed to Ohio State to contribute to the team's success at the highest level possible, but the problem was that my body—my knees—didn't allow me to do that. Not being able to play the way I believed I could was devastating! I didn't know where the road was taking me, and doubts about my future as a Buckeye crept in; mentally, I was still beaten up pretty badly, and I'd reached the lowest point in my life. I'd played football for 20 years, and that's all I knew. Though I did my best to maintain a smile and a positive attitude outwardly, I didn't like my situation. Mentally, I struggled in silence.

For the first time in my life, I wasn't certain whether I wanted to continue playing at Ohio State or if I even wanted to continue playing football at all. The thought itself was depressing. It all became stale for about two weeks, and the level of stress and anxiety got so heavy that it became something I'd never experienced. Trying to be strong, I attempted to face it alone, but I only made it worse.

The thing is, this wasn't something I could prevent. I was changing. I became negative, which wasn't my nature, and started complaining about everything, including the most insignificant things. I was rooted in an unhealthy place and constantly grumpy, but I didn't think anyone noticed because I'd laugh it off when I was in a bad mood. Laughter kept others from seeing or feeling my pain. Laughter was the distraction that kept people from knowing I needed something.

As a compromise, to at least try to continue playing since the transfer portal wasn't as friendly to us at the time, I thought of dropping down in my division. If I did, at least I could transfer and play immediately. Playing football was all I knew and the only thing I'd ever done. That was my job. I became discouraged, but it didn't have anything to do with the university, the coaches, or my teammates—that was as good as it gets.

In the end, I decided that I wanted a fresh start. By the end of 2016, flipping over to 2017, I left the team after bowl season as a self-preservation technique, but could feel in my soul that it wasn't the right decision. It was still light out when I got home from my classes, and I would sit alone in my place, contemplating the future and my life. I was no longer a football player, and I didn't know what it was like to just be Johnnie. I didn't see the guys every day, and I wasn't in that brotherhood anymore because our schedules didn't align. I didn't know what the hell to do with myself. I got stuck in my head, overthinking, overwhelmed, and uncertain. It wasn't a good place to be.

A big part of my struggle was coming to terms with the understanding that my lifelong goal was no longer possible. I carried myself as a leader on the field because I learned that who you are follows you. That introduction is there before people get to know you. Given that my teammates expected a leader to be confident, able to handle adversity, a hard worker, and make wise decisions under pressure, I thought it was best to internalize everything and keep pushing, but it deepened my depression. For a kid who played football their entire life, what else was there? There was nothing left for me.

I had a plan from the time I was young when most people still don't care which direction they're going. But I knew: get myself and my mother out of the hood. Football was the only option. If I failed, I failed my mother, too. When I thought about the shootings back home, where she was, I was the solution to get her out of that. I'd lost too many people already in the hood, and it wasn't safe for her or my siblings.

Aside from therapy, I met with Coach Meyer, Coach Day, and other football staff. They listened, understood what I was feeling, and showed support. The coaches and their staff encouraged me to give football another shot before making a decision that would affect my career.

Bobby Carpenter, Brian Hartline, a former receiver for the Buckeyes fresh out of the Browns, and legend Zac Boren didn't know me, but as leaders would do, in a super dope way, they were encouraging and, unknowingly, their support kept me at Ohio State University. Brian checked on me every day, and before I returned, he still called to check on me when I was struggling in school. Although I was a good student prior to college, it was different. I struggled in several areas because mentally, I wasn't where I needed to be.

I don't think I could have made it out of that space alone. Having people in my corner was essential. I wouldn't have gone back if I didn't have anyone encourage me to try.

Parris Campbell called me daily, telling me, "We need you back."

"I don't know if I'll be back playing ball," I told him, "but I'll help out."

For some reason, Parris didn't give up, and he became a huge reason I returned. People want and need to be acknowledged when they're struggling with things, and my brothers let me know I mattered. They reminded me why I needed to keep going. I signed on the dotted line, I wanted to finish what I had committed to.

When I returned, my brothers and the coaches made me feel as though they needed me, and I needed to battle back. I had to finish my journey of helping some of the younger guys behind us become leaders. Terry McLaurin and Parris continued to help me with that, and we rode that thing out. I was a supporting cast member for those two. Though I was a little older than Terry and Parris, I looked up to them.

When I say you never know what someone is going through, you don't. When Parris came to Ohio State, he was only 16, playing on a team with older guys. As one of the youngest players, if not *the* youngest, Parris was subjected to things at the Ohio State University he couldn't have prepared for. We had a conversation about what I went through, and Parris opened up about his own struggles.

"JD," that's what Parris called me, "when I was a freshman, I battled depression, too. It was serious. I went from being the best at my high school to the Ohio State. It was humbling to be at a place where everyone could do what I could do and do it better! These were 19- and 20-year-olds coming in with me. It was a little bit of a shock. It had me wondering how I was going to keep up. I was redshirted and until that point, it was the roughest part of my life. I called Mom and Grandma and told them, 'This isn't working. I need to go home or transfer.'

"Three or four games in, I was heading to study hall, and I was on the phone with my mom. I told her everything going on with me and I was bawling my eyes out! I couldn't sleep because I was having these crazy dreams. Super dark stuff. Driving to the facility and it was burning; I was in a car accident; Traveling to an away game and the plane would crash. I wasn't able to sleep because of this. Now, Mom had sympathy for me but while I was huffing and puffing, she put it in a different perspective. She said, 'Parris, stop! Stop!' I asked, 'What do you mean? I can't!' Mom said, 'This is not you.' It wasn't what I wanted to hear.

"I had just turned 17 at that point, and I was dealing with depression. Hearing my mom say that didn't sound like the most caring advice. But she was reassuring me that yes, you are going through a dark time, and this isn't what you wanted, but you have to realize who you are and what you are destined to be." he sighed. "JD, the year was still rough, but I kept talking to her and working to get better. Eventually, it shifted my focus. To get better you have to actively *work* to get better. This meant I had to change my mental state. Somehow, I needed to turn that darkness or fear off mentally."

Although Parris didn't see a therapist or take advantage of the support at Ohio State we had access to, he did start opening up to his mom who helped him work through it. He also had someone he came into Ohio State with who he could talk to when he got stuck in a dark place. Talking to Parris made me realize that running into depression as an athlete is more common than many of us assume. It can feel like we're going through these things alone, but we're not standing far away from someone else who is also going through it.

Parris could see what I was going through when many other people didn't see it because he had gone through it, too. He told me that when I didn't want to be around the facility or the game itself, he sensed something was off.

If you know someone well enough, you can tell when they're not themselves. They become standoffish. For example, if you're in conversation with an eager talker and one of their triggers comes up, they don't want to talk. I was always in tune with my surroundings. I could read people and sense when their energy changed. I'm usually happy, but when depression hit me, I changed. I stayed in my dorm room and kept to myself. We never want to mitigate anyone's depression because what people go through and how they experience it is different.

Football was my escape from life outside of it. It was how I expressed and worked out negative emotions. No one walks away from the single thing they love most without there being a serious reason.

When I look back on my life, I realized anxiety had been showing up for a long time. I just didn't know it because I was in it so much. I immediately felt it my responsibility to get out and make a name for myself. I felt my responsibility to be able to get my mom out of the hood and give my whole family a better life. That was a constant, flowing undercurrent that never shut off.

I knew therapy was working. Each time I left the therapist, a guy with a ponytail who looked like Steven Segal had provided a safe space to release what was blocking my progress and what I didn't understand to the point that I'd breathe a sigh of relief. I felt free from what I was carrying.

Over time, therapy helped me prepare for whatever was thrown at me by becoming better equipped to receive it. By that time, I had the motivation, and it all clicked. I understood why I had depression and the reasons it was essential to get the professional support I needed. The pain of loss, the inability to pursue my goals, the threat of having it all end because of an injury in my junior year of high school, and losing the opportunity to get Mama out of the hood—a self-imposed burden I silently carried—were contributors to the overwhelming guilt mounting inside of me. And this one football game, the contributions, and the brotherhood that naturally came with it was something that nothing else could give me. I needed to see all of the work I'd put in for more than 20 years prior come to fruition.

Stewie was a constant source of inspiration, pushing me harder than ever. And therapy helped lift me over the hump. All I needed to do was talk to someone outside of my network, unbiased, with no emotional attachment, to tell me what I may have wanted to hear.

As an athlete, I was never prepared for an injury. As a human being, I wasn't prepared for so much death. I wasn't afraid of adversity, and I didn't have any doubts about things not working out, but like J. Cole said, "There's beauty in the struggle."

I knew my purpose was bigger than football. God put me here for a reason, and I had to get my mental health together and heal to meet the challenges and opportunities ahead of me. I wasn't in a place to fully help anyone while I was addressing my depression, so I continued with therapy with a new drive.

---

**THAT SUMMER, BEGINNING MY** fourth year, Viv packed up and moved from Arizona to Ohio in a leap of faith. I was back on track with football, finally able to contribute to the team. Although a hamstring pull caused me to miss a game as a precaution, I played the rest of the season without missing any practices or games.

The first play of the Penn State game was huge! Saquon Barkley ran a kick return back 97 yards for a touchdown, and if something like that happens, it will be a long night. They were up, and we battled the whole game. I scored my first touchdown in the third quarter, and with four or five minutes left, I caught another touchdown. That was the loudest I'd ever heard the 'Shoe (the Buckeye stadium, the Horseshoe).

We came back a drive or two later when JT Barrett hit Marcus Baugh, our tight end, for another touchdown. That revenge game was the biggest game of the season. The brotherhood was insane! To see how we, the whole team, pulled together for a 39-38 win was unforgettable. Our defense was spectacular. JT Barrett played one hell of a fourth quarter with 16 passes in a row and three touchdowns in the fourth quarter. We won a Big Ten Championship against the Wisconsin Badgers and the Cotton Bowl Classic against USC, but Penn State was *the* game.

I got into a different bag with my studies and buckled down. Parris and I took statistics together, which would have been the class to stop me, but I turned my last year into my most successful academically. I started my first year as a communication major, which lasted only three weeks. Intuitively, coupled with football, I wanted to do something to help people, so I'd changed my major to Sociology. I had to take academics more seriously because I couldn't play in the bowl games if I didn't graduate. And since I came in early, I was running out of time, aware I wouldn't return to school after playing. I focused and finished, graduating in December 2018 with a bachelor's in Sociology.

Despite the personal and physical challenges I fought to overcome, I ended that fifth season with 42 receptions for 669 yards. I had eight touchdowns, which placed me 11th in Ohio State history with 16 touchdown receptions, including one in each of my final three games, which we won, against Michigan in the regular season, Northwestern in the Big Ten championship game, and Washington in the Rose Bowl.

Some of the players came to me for advice about things they were struggling with after seeing me overcome my own battles, even one of the soccer players. I had candid conversations with them to help in any way I could. They were all working toward big goals while trying to figure out life and all its ups and downs. In my last year, a group of black athletes started Redefining Athletic Standards (RAS). Encompassing black athletes from all sports, RAS did community service and had group meetings with our Athletic Director, Gene Smith, to discuss mental health and what we needed to see around campus.

I wouldn't have learned to invest in others that way without the guys who came before me—those who did that for me. People often see the big plays and big wins, but football is more than a game. No one was obligated to encourage and inspire me, but some individuals walked or intersected my path and left a significant impact because they wanted me to win in life, not just in the game. It showed me that caring for people is the best thing you can do in this life because everything else can fade away.

# JOHNN(IE)

## FORGE • AHEAD

**IN THE EARLY DAYS,** *gridiron became a term that became synonymous with American football. Originally, the term came to fruition due to the football field lines resembling a gridiron cooking grate with parallel bars used for grilling food over an open flame. Oftentimes football players, and athletes in general, feel as if they truly are playing over an open flame in regard to their mental state and the heat they feel to perform at their absolute best on a daily basis. Isolation can be dangerous and every day I'm thankful for Parris and my brothers who would not allow me to quit.*

*It can be challenging to encourage a friend to continue going and you may not be quite sure on how to even approach that conversation. I'm sure Parris sharing his struggles was extremely hard for him; however, his vulnerability allowed me to open up more. This allowed us to lean on each other, creating a brotherhood that most people only saw on the gridiron. You may have a friend* reading this who is struggling mentally and you're not quite sure how to approach the conversation. Approaching a friend who may be struggling mentally requires sensitivity, empathy, and support. Here are a few tips to help you navigate the conversation:

- **EXPRESS CONCERN AND CARE**: Approach your friend with empathy and compassion, expressing genuine concern for their well-being. Use empathetic language and let them know that you're there to listen and support them.

- **BE A GOOD LISTENER & PRAY**: It goes without saying—listen. Intently listen without judgment or interruption. Listen actively, validate their feelings, and show empathy and understanding. Offer to pray for peace and guidance as they navigate their current adversities.

- **ASK OPEN-ENDED QUESTIONS**: Encourage your friend to share their thoughts and feelings by asking open-ended questions. Start the conversation by asking:
  - Why...
  - How...
  - What...

o   *Describe/Explain...*

- **ENCOURAGE PROFESSIONAL HELP**: *If your friend's mental health concerns seem severe or persistent, gently encourage them to seek professional help with a therapist, counselor, or mental health professional. Offer to assist them in locating a professional or setting the appointment for them.*

- **FOLLOW-UP**: *Be sure to check in regularly to see how they're doing and offer ongoing support. Let them know you will be there for them, and they can reach you at any time.*

*Approaching a friend who may be struggling mentally can be challenging, but by showing empathy, support, and understanding, you can help them feel heard, valued, and supported just as my teammates did for me during some of the darkest times of my life.*

*Parris, thank you.*

# GRID(IRON)

# land(mines)

## JOHNN(Y)

**TO GET THROUGH ANY** adversity, you have to recenter yourself around your "why." When we first arrived in Iraq, the tone of command was to "Win the hearts and minds of the people." Unfortunately, a harsh reality taught me that's not what we do. Maybe the National Guard and the Army can win the hearts and minds of the people, but if terrorists were going to cause us mass destruction and pain, we were there to return the favor. Our 2/7 motto was to "cry havoc and let slip the dogs of war," however, we all felt we were being contained instead of doing what we were trained to do.

The Marines taught us one thing, winning, and that's all we wanted to do. On our initial patrols, they wanted us to wave at people and pass out soccer balls and candy. Even though a lot of us were confused and agitated by the orders, we did it. We made the mistake of being nice and social, then the first person in our company was killed, Corporal David Vicente.

The day David was killed, we'd just recently talked about being home and just how different Iraq is in general. Nothing too deep. Just small talk; how the living standards sucked and that poking a hole in the top of a water bottle just to shower wasn't the life we signed up for. The Army had great Up-Armored Humvees that could withstand explosions better, but our Humvees were the worst of the worst. We had to zip-tie Kevlar blankets to the sides for added protection because there wasn't anything, and if the Humvee had doors, we were lucky! If we had better Humvees, a few of our guys would be here today. Well, that night a patrol went out, and one of the Humvees got stuck in the mud. David and his squad were sent out as the Quick Reaction Force (QRF) to assist and retrieve the Humvee, but their vehicle hit a landmine.

That night changed all of us. Sitting outside, a lot of commotion began in the command center, so I ran down to see what was happening. We heard, "Confirmed one KIA, Repeat, one KIA." Per protocol, we never gave names over the radio, but since we didn't know who was killed, we started running through the names of anyone outside the wire. Our corpsman darted out of there and raced over to the medical center to begin prepping for the injured, but I could do nothing to help them. I stood on the second-floor balcony as they pulled the Humvee into the gate, towing the severely damaged vehicle David was in behind it.

That was the first time I experienced death. At that point, I hadn't lost anyone in my family or even been to a funeral. But I stood there watching the corpsman slowly drag a black body bag out of the back of the Humvee. Blood was pouring from the corners onto the gravel and pavement. My eyes locked on the bag, and I thought it was just a matter of time before I'd be in one of them. I believe most of us had that same thought, only my logic didn't derive from fear; it was reality.

There's silence, and then there's a level of quietness beyond silence. As they dragged David's body off the back of the Humvee, that was the greatest silence I have ever known. I knew the Marines had prepared us for war; up to that point, I'd trained thousands of hours! But I wasn't prepared for the emotional and mental devastation war causes, and certainly not the loss of life that comes with combat.

Walking into our squad bay, I sat down on a meal ready-to-eat (MRE) box to take a break, picking up a Gatorade and granola bar, when I noticed an index card on the floor. I swear I stared at it for about five minutes before picking it up. I pulled a pen from the flak jacket resting near my feet and wrote "FEAR" on one side of the index card, flipped it over and wrote "WHY" on the other. Under FEAR, I wrote down three things:

1. *DEATH*
2. *Letting my MEN down*
3. *Letting MYSELF down*

After David's death, those three things consumed my thoughts, pushing me to train every day just to avoid my fears. Under WHY, I wrote three more things:

1. *For FREEDOM*
2. *For my FAMILY*
3. *For my COUNTRY*

And knowing I could only say yes to one side of that card, I committed to saying yes to the why.

Being in Iraq, we were already surrounded by combat and death, and in a place of fear. But David's death changed our mindset, and we shifted from "Win the hearts and minds" to "No better friend, no worse enemy." We took ourselves as no worse enemy. Some Marines started saying, "Two in the heart, one in the mind," which meant if they were going to blow us up, we'd put it to them. The only problem with that philosophy was that we never saw the enemy because they were too cowardly to face us. Our survival depended on us.

I knew we had to do things differently when I became a team leader. Our squad started stopping in the most populated areas wearing a mask or face paint, sprinting out of the Humvees, sliding on our knees, yelling "Set!"

When the locals started noticing how we carried ourselves, they were afraid and knew not to mess with us. Every time, we made it a point to respond in a tone that would intimidate anyone around us. One of the

Sheiks even asked our Captain, "What unit do you have here that is different?"

We were so intimidating that they thought we were acting alone, separate from the unit. I truly believe acting this way might have saved us. The word was, "You'd better let that platoon go because they might kill everyone." We weren't to be taken lightly. If the enemy wanted to blend in, we made sure that we didn't. The problem with creating a process toward success is that once there's a little bit of adversity and pain, people abandon it. But we didn't. We couldn't!

I knew it was impossible to say yes to my fear and my why. So, I checked my mental status before every training exercise or operation. I went to the gym to get a workout and read the card aloud, asking myself, "After this workout, which way are you moving? Towards your fear, or why?" Before every mission, I'd pull the index card from my flak jacket and ask myself that same question. Then, I'd flip the card over and read each of my fears and why, committing to saying "yes" to my why. I worked and trained harder if I didn't feel I was accomplishing my why.

I still keep that card close. It's in my nightstand drawer.

The largest danger we constantly faced was never from an enemy we could see but rather from an enemy we couldn't see. We were far more fearful of a landmine hidden beneath the sand than we were of an ambush or enemy contact by gunfire. We *wanted* the enemy to challenge us with gunfire. We thrived on waiting for the enemy to face us. What we got instead was the daily fear of Russian Roulette, driving around until an explosion occurred.

When a landmine or an IED is triggered, there is nothing you can do. In an instant, your life could be over or forever changed. It was the fear of the unknown that kept me up at night. When David was killed by running over a landmine, it changed my mindset—it forced me to create a mental standard that I still carry today, focusing on my purpose and my why." Without that moment of adversity, I might not have created an index card that would carry me through some of the darkest moments of my life and still carries me today.

In 2004, when we traveled to Fallujah, that simple concept, my why—for freedom, my family, and country—made me mentally stronger for myself and my men. Going into Fallujah was our Super Bowl. We felt prepared for whatever was ahead of us, and mentally I was in a different place to lead my men without the fear of death. I'd already accepted that I could die but knew I had to focus on my why to come out alive.

There's a level of fear that most people will never experience, like when we had to kick in a door in the middle of Fallujah and pray that there wasn't someone on the other side waiting for us with an AK-47. In my mind, there was only one way to overcome that fear: to have a why. My team—Dew, Fortune, and Clevenger, the men to my left and right, were my why. And even if I was scared, I was their leader. I wanted to lead by example by going through every door first.

After traveling back to Hit, we would often take our Captain to other bases around the region for joint meetings with the higher ups. On one of our trips we re-fueled, ate some chow, and went to the Post Exchange (PX) as the Captain was discussing offensive operations within the region. One of the guys bought a Marine Corps Times, so I grabbed it and began flipping through the pages reading articles until I saw a face I'd never forget. I was in shock.

The article read Lance Corporal Jonathan Collins, KIA 8.08.2004. Jon—my best friend at the School of Infantry in San Diego. I later heard the details from Davidson who was with him when it happened. He said Jon was killed in Ramadi by an enemy sniper while on post. What's unfortunate is that about two to three weeks after his death, we received brand new Kevlar that might have saved his life.

I can't express how much regret I felt at that moment. Jon was the best man and Marine I've ever met, and he was gone at 19. I felt I'd let Jon and Davidson down because I was supposed to be with them—to lead them. The Marines taught us not to love or feel, as a survival tactic, and what little I had left came out when Jon was killed. I broke.

I felt hate boiling inside of me. I had anger, fear, and resentment—I hated everything about Iraq. I even started questioning God. *Why would God do this to 19-year-old men? Why would human beings commit such hatred towards each other?* I became numb to life, death—hell, everything!

# LAND(MINES)

Being numb made me a better Marine. The problem was that I lost my sense of self and faith in the process. There's always something that can challenge what we believe in, and Iraq did that for me. My heart was hardening, and resentment was the glue.

Some of the things I saw or experienced, I can't forget. I've got a lot of examples, but on this particularly sweltering day on Route Page, we had some action. A little boy, no more than ten years old, wearing a pair of worn sandals, a white thobe with brown cloth tied around his waist, jet-black hair, and brown eyes. He had a head wrap hanging around his neck; it wasn't on his head. He was walking his sheep about 500 yards away from our post. I was watching him through the scope of my ACOG on my rifle, ensuring he wasn't trying to plant an IED. The locals were known for using children against us. Think about that. *Children!* So, you know we couldn't trust anyone because everything was a matter of life and death.

Eventually the boy walked off, appearing not to be a threat.

The next day, around the same time, the little boy herding his sheep showed up again, wearing the same clothes. He got a little closer, so I spoke up and told Corporal Black I was taking my team down to talk to him. Black shrugged it off but nodded, indicating that talking to him was okay. Consequently, knowing complacency kills, I cautiously approached the boy with my team, but he didn't seem to be a threat.

"Asa-lama Lakum," I said.

The boy responded, "Lakum Salam."

"Isme, Johnny."

"Isme, Mohammad." That was all the Arabic I knew at the time, so I thought, *what now?* I tried asking Mohammad what he was doing, but he started making helicopter noises and gun sounds. I didn't understand what he was trying to say, so I took out my pocket notebook with a pencil and drew sheep. I then gave it to Mohammad, and he drew a picture. Once we began communicating through pictures, he drew a stick figure shooting down a helicopter on one page, flipped to the next page, and drew explosions and the shape of a rocket-propelled grenade (RPG). Looking at his pictures, I was certain that Mohammad was trying to warn us about something, but I couldn't understand what he was attempting to convey.

In the best way I could, I told him to come back the next day, hopeful he understood and would return. When we got back to the observation post (OP), I explained to Corporal Black what happened and requested to have a translator sent out to us. A translator came out the next day—and so did Mohammad. I saw this brave little boy just three times, and he led our unit to the largest weapons cache discovered in all of Al-Anbar Provence at the time. They were buried less than three miles from our FOB, under a water tower that we stared at every day from our base.

It took 17 seven-ton military trucks to retrieve the weapons, explosives, and ammunition. This kid didn't want to see war or death. Mohammad didn't know me, but somehow, he knew their intent wasn't good. I couldn't imagine the courage it took him to tell us where those weapons were. I believe that Mohammad might have saved my life and the lives of several Marines and military personnel who traveled along Route Bronze, one of Iraq's most dangerous supply routes.

I thought about Mohammad every day but never saw him herding sheep again. I knew his family received money from the discovery, but I wasn't privy to how much. A few weeks passed, and one of the lieutenants came to me and asked if I remembered the boy who led us to the weapons cache. When I told him, "Yes, Mohammad," the lieutenant said he had been killed, along with his family.

When he told me, the conversation became a blurred memory. I don't think I said anything. I walked away and just cried. That was the pain flushing out because a huge part of me began to shift. I hated being in Iraq.

That boy gave his life so we could protect our supply route. I believed that if we weren't there, we wouldn't need a supply route in the first place. The numbness I already felt about death deepened. I didn't care if I died. First David Vicente, then Jon, and now this innocent little boy. Corporal Black received the credit for discovering the weapons cache, earning the Navy and Marine Corps Achievement Medal. I'm sure our lieutenant and captain also received a medal.

My team and I didn't get a medal, but I didn't care about that. Mohammad was gone, and so was a part of me. No medal would ever replace the sacrifice Mohammad made.

David Vicente, Jon, and Mohammad became a part of my why. As did Lance Corporal Aric Barr, killed in April of 2004, and Lance Corporal Kane Funke, who was killed a week after Jon. These men were in our company, and I knew them very closely. Vicente, my buddy Jon, and Mohammad motivated me to do everything I could to better protect my squad and anyone under my leadership. And when it comes to leadership, not everyone knows how to lead or even cares about where they're leading people. Great leaders don't just lead by example; they help those they're leading develop strong leadership qualities as well.

One of the morale daggers we experienced was when our command decided that the potholes from all the IEDs along Route Bronze were becoming an eyesore for the locals. The command offered to fill the holes with concrete as a symbol of collaboration with the city of Hit and to gain the local community's trust. So here we are acting as a road construction crew, filling in the very holes that reminded us of the explosions aimed at taking our lives. From the start, I knew it was a bad idea and voiced my opinion to Corporal Black. Corporal Black hated it when I spoke up because even though he knew I was right, it wouldn't change anything.

It didn't take much intelligence to understand that if the enemy were to watch us begin filling potholes with concrete, they could easily place an IED inside an existing IED hole and just wait for us to patch it. Common sense. The command requested three combat engineers, who traveled to Fallujah with us, to fill in the potholes using Quikrete, and ours was to secure the area and hold security for 24 hours to allow the concrete to set. They didn't want insurgents placing IEDs in wet concrete.

Third Platoon was on rotation to take the combat engineers out to fill holes. The engineers backed their Humvee up to the existing IED hole, and Corporal Dominique Nicolas jumped out wearing his black jungle boots. He was the most knowledgeable Marine I'd ever met when it came to explosives. Originally from South Africa, Corporal Nicolas mentioned that he fought in the British Royal Marines prior to becoming a U.S. Marine.

# LAND(MINES)

He pulled a bag of Quikrete out of the back and jumped into the IED hole.

"Shit! There's an IED in here!" was heard over the radio. Then—*BOOM!* The blast killed all three of the engineers. No one was identifiable. Only body parts and a black pair of boots were discovered, along with the torsos inside their flak jackets. Our platoon was tasked with taking the bodies to the morgue at Camp Al Asad. The body parts were placed into old MRE boxes and thrown into the back of our Humvees, along with their personal items. We were disposable.

I became friends with a combat engineer, Corporal Matt Henderson. Anyone who knew him called him Hendu. I got to know him when the engineers were attached to our unit for Operation Vigilant Resolve through Fallujah. Then, a month later, he was gone. After Jon and Hendu—I realized it was better not to have friends in the Marine Corps.

Every day I tried to understand it because I didn't deserve to live any more than they deserved to die. Every day I wished I could have traded places with them. After the engineers were killed, we took black spray-paint and wrote "COMPLACENCY KILLS" all over the base, so no one would miss it when they left the barbed wire. It was a harsh reminder that we must be vigilant for ourselves and each other every day. In the Marines, those details became the difference between life and death. War is volatile. Some weeks nothing happened, and I felt like the enemy just completely forgot we existed. Then, in other weeks, everything seemed to go wrong.

I started questioning everything we did. There wasn't accountability for poor guidance and the decisions that caused their deaths. Even when we got to the morgue, the military personnel working there were selling DVDs, magazines, PlayStations, TVs, and other personal items of those killed in combat. I was fuming at their lack of respect and didn't hold back the few choice words I had for them. I wanted to knock them out for selling our brothers' stuff! They stayed in comfortable tents on a well-secured base with Subway and Burger King. We lost three dedicated Marines because our command ordered them to fill potholes! Even after their deaths, it didn't stop. They kept sending us right back out there to find IEDs at night, not expecting us to return.

# LAND(MINES)

One night while on foot patrol, Hackler from our squad found a daisy chain of eight IEDs by tripping over a buried 155mm artillery shell. We were thankful it didn't go off, or all 13 of us would have been killed instantly. Observing the surroundings caused me to become less fearful of the enemy and more fearful of our own people. The trauma was ongoing, but I could function normally because that's how we were built. While the Marines had removed emotions detrimental to our focus, two remained, and I was filled with them—hate and anger. It didn't take long to figure out that war is hell and only the dead see the end of war.

I understood that the command was receiving orders from a higher command, and those were likely given to him by an even higher command. But for the guys on the ground, we thought it was only a matter of time until we got the order that would end our lives, most likely due to a lack of common sense.

I blamed God, mostly because I couldn't blame anyone or anything else at the time. I started resenting God, then basically became an atheist, believing if there was a God, why would He put us in hell like this? And why would He treat the children of the world the way we were being treated? It pained me that there was nothing we could do about it. I came to the conclusion that I would die in Iraq. It may have been a subconscious coping mechanism. But, man, as I walked past a trash can on the way back to the Humvee, I ripped open the Velcro of my flak jacket, and pulled out the worn and torn desert camouflaged Bible the chaplain gave me in Kuwait when I was baptized. After staring at it for a few seconds, I closed my eyes and threw it in the trash can.

After what I had experienced, my faith had eroded. At that time, I believed if God was going to leave us to die in that forsaken country, then there was no God, so I'd take my fate in my own hands.

I know God never lost His faith in me. He waited for me to go through the journey I needed to become who I am today. He's always waiting. But sometimes, when people lose something, it can take time to get it back.

# LAND(MINES)

## FORGE • AHEAD

**EVERY DAY WE ALL** *face landmines hidden beneath the surface, just waiting for us to step on the pressure plate. We face landmines such as job loss, divorce, questions of faith, death, anxiety, and depression. The trigger is an instant explosion that rattles our life and shakes our mental fortitude to its core. As Marines, we spent hours upon hours training for what happens after a landmine explodes. How do you dismount? Who is taking care of the casualties? Where do you set up defensive positions in a way to not cause more harm? These are all questions and scenarios that you have to train to the point of muscle memory.*

*However, in our own lives we do not prepare for landmines mentally; instead, we navigate life as if we will never face any adversity. How you prepare for those landmines during your times of calmness is how you create the mental fortitude to survive when they explode. Here are some strategies I have discovered over the years that* help me prepare for the many landmines that we could face in life:

- **FAITH**: Having a strong faith and foundation built upon a relationship with Christ has given me strength in times of adversity. Focusing on your daily prayers and devotions will create a strong foundation in which you can stand upon during times of trials.

- **SELF-TALK**: One of my favorite YouTube channels is Ben Lionel Scott's. There are several motivational videos that I bookmark and listen to during times of adversity to provide a state of self-talk to build confidence.

- **EXERCISE**: Creating a weekly workout routine gives you the space to find clarity and a sense of accomplishment. Creating a routine will allow you to continue your workouts during times of adversity as a stress release.

- **NATURE**: My place of refuge is the woods. I find peace whether in a tree stand or simply walking through the woods. Listening and feeling the harmony of nature allows me to recenter my emotions while reducing stress. Find a place of refuge. A place to meditate.

- **WHY VS. FEAR:** Creating your "why" and understanding your fears could be the single greatest exercise you do. You can only create your WHY, if you understand your FEARS. Write down your FEARS and then create your WHY. Every day you have a choice to answer yes to one.

Reviewing the adversities you have faced can help you create the mental resilience needed to survive any landmine that you could face in the future.

Mohammad, thank you.

# forge(d)

## JOHNN(IE)

**THE ROSE BOWL WAS** Coach Meyer's last game as the Ohio State University Head Football Coach, and the next part of my career started the following day: getting ready for the NFL Combine training. It was pretty dope. Viv and I moved the day after the Rose Bowl, choosing Arizona as the place to train since her parents were there. Besides, I had a nice time when we went back and having met Viv after the Fiesta Bowl it was a special place. Parris wanted to train out there, too, and having my best friend with me on that part of the journey couldn't get any better.

The NFL Combine was in Indianapolis in the Colts stadium, and I couldn't wait to put in the work. All the top executives, coaching staff, player personnel, and even medical staff from all 32 NFL teams were there to evaluate the top college football players eligible for the draft. The way I saw it, this was my job interview to showcase all my years of work to play in the NFL.

Our training group was comprised of hardworking guys, and when that extra discipline called, we went twice a day. The coaches didn't play either; they pushed us to the max. Not our max—the max. Bench press max. 40-yard max. Vertical jump max. Broad jump max. Everything. I had my 40-yard dash time at 4.41 seconds. I gave it everything I had.

The way other athletes watered it down made it seem like the Combine wasn't hard. With so much at stake, I worked my butt off to exhaustion. Parris and I were ready for the NFL Combine's intense and motivating atmosphere. I met AJ Brown, DK Metcalf, and many others. It was impressive to see their preparation because I found that some didn't take it seriously. This was the next level! Everything had to go into the Combine. I couldn't leave anything out. I was there for four days, grinding, interviewing, completing physicals, and performing on the last day. Terry, Parris, and I killed the Combine! My agent, Jason Bernstein, was checking on me to make sure the goals I set were coming together. All I did was focus.

Holding it down while I was on this journey, Viv was nothing but supportive. I'd just gotten to the field, about to start our route session one morning, when I got the call that Viv was in the hospital. She was in labor with our daughter Zya. When I found out I was going to be a father, I was excited. I'd always wanted to be a dad someday. I raised my brother and sister and was ready to have kids of my own who would look up to me. I wanted to be able to do good for my children and provide for them. I was determined to be a different father than my dad was to me.

---

IT'S NOT A COINCIDENCE when you meet certain people. You instinctively know that it's someone you want in your life. Around the time of the NFL Combine, Kato Mitchell connected me with Johnny Dawson. Kato and his wife, Viv and I, and another couple had dinner with Johnny and his wife, Borah. Borah was incredibly hands-on with Zya during the dinner and seemed like a really good and loving mother to their four children. From day one, I found them to be good people. Johnny seemed to have a wealth of experiences to share. Although we didn't exchange stories or dive too deep into conversation about ourselves that night, he was kind, knowledgeable, and genuine. Something about Johnny told me that he cared about people.

I was big into watching *Forged in Fire*, a knife show. Sometime after the dinner, I posted on Instagram that I wanted to make a knife. Johnny hit me up and said he'd found a guy that made knives and could teach me how to do it, so he went with me on the adventure. I was going to try something I'd been thinking about for months now.

Forging a knife means shaping a piece of steel to create a sharpened blade, and it takes patience. As we began the forging process to make our own knives, the temperature had to reach 2,200 degrees Fahrenheit to create a red glow over the small piece of steel. Once the metal reached the proper temperature, we removed the steel from the forge and placed it on an anvil to begin the shaping process. We used large hammers to strike the metal repeatedly to compress and then reshape the steel into a blade. After shaping, we cooled the steel to ensure its strength and prevent it from becoming too brittle. Once the blade was shaped and cooled, we began the sharpening process while polishing and etching the final product.

We had a great time together. It was the start of discovering just how much we had in common, including our faith and share of adversity, despite our vastly different lives. Johnny didn't want anything from me. If we made knives and then parted ways, he was cool, and so was I, but there was something more to him that ran deeper and with purpose.

I tapped into Johnny's highly competitive side when he told me that he had brought his guns. After we made the knives, waiting for them to firm up, we took a little gun break and did some shooting.

"JD, you can't hit that target all the way out there with that handgun," he said, nodding at the target. I think he wanted to see if I had any skills with a gun. Then he heard, "Bing!"

"Give me my money," I joked, showing off my clay shooting skills, and we broke out in laughter.

After having so much fun together, I introduced Johnny to my little brother and cousin, and we went out shooting again. My family got to know him over time, and they liked him, too.

---

**DESPITE MY INJURIES, I'D** been healthy for two years, with two great years on the field. After crushing it in the Combine, one of my favorite receivers, Steve Smith, said, "You've got to watch out for this kid, Johnnie Dixon."

There were whispers about how well I was running my routes. Although I didn't think I would go in the first few rounds of the NFL draft or know who would sign me, I believed someone would draft me. My agent and I were confident it would happen and thought the possibility of going in round three or four was realistic. I had been waiting for this and was ready to prove myself even more!

On the first day of the NFL Draft, I went to celebrate the momentous occasion with Parris. He had an Airbnb and had invited all his friends. We all figured he'd go in the first round since he had 90 catches for 1,063 yards and 12 touchdowns, but that didn't happen. Parris was pissed at the end of the night and went to be by himself to let off some steam. I knew he'd get drafted in the second round the following day, though. There's no way Parris would go below that. He got the call in the second round and 59 overall, drafted by the Colts. That was his special moment, and he earned it. I was happy for Parris and proud of him because he was an incredible player.

Since I knew I wasn't going in round one or two, I was waiting for my turn to come after Parris had his.

Mama, Uncle Dante (Mama's younger brother), and my cousin Pat came up to wait on the results with us. My cousin had an Airbnb and we watched the draft there. On the third day, which is the longest, we had approximately 20 people watching with us, including Johnny, Borah, and their kids. Parris and Kato were there, too—everybody was happy and excited for me as we waited for my name to get called and scroll across the ticker at the bottom of the screen.

A couple more receivers were drafted. Terry McLaurin went in the third round, and I thought I'd be close in the fourth, especially after receiving calls and text messages from several teams. The Ravens were among them, so I couldn't help but remain optimistic.

Watching some of the guys being drafted while I was still waiting rendered Parris and me at a loss. We knew I should have been drafted before them. The Colts called and said they might take me in the sixth round, but they didn't pick me up. Then some other teams called and said, "If you don't get drafted, we'll get you as a free agent." I didn't want to hear that, so my standard reply was, "Call me after this is over."

When it got late, Parris was doing everything to keep my mind off the fact that I hadn't been drafted. Watching the screen was discouraging and I was upset. Then the last pick came. My name wasn't called.

My agent called and told me that we'd figure out my options and the best teams to go to. I tried to keep it together, but I noticed Mama had slipped outside. I imagine it was because she was crying. Playing football was never just about me. It was about seeing dreams come true for my family as well. My mother had always been there for me—when I committed to Ohio State, my battles with my knees, the frustration with not playing, everything. What I felt, she felt That night probably hurt Mama more than it hurt me, and seeing my mother cry messed me up.

I continued speaking with my agent and various teams, including the Houston Texans throughout the night. Ten minutes before the draft was over, I signed with Houston as a free agent. I felt a little better to be going to a team. However, I was still pissed off because I killed the Combine and Pro Day, so being drafted just seemed like a given.

When Mama returned, I walked over and told her, "Mama, we good. We good!" I told her I had signed with Houston. She wrapped her arms around my neck, hugging me so tightly I thought she was about to break it.

Mama knew most of what I had to overcome and how I finished my last two years. She didn't hold back her tears. She was hurt and angry that my potential wasn't seen. She saw my passion and knew the years of work I'd put in to get to the NFL.

I ended the night bowling with Johnny and his sons since it was somewhat therapeutic. Johnny came over and gave me a motivational lift, reminding me not to give up on my dream.

"It isn't over. You know you've worked hard. Push through," he said. To make sure I understood what he meant, Johnny looked me in the eyes firmly and stated as though it was a directive, "Bro, listen. Don't allow any of this to deter you from your dream. Keep going—God's got you." He knew what was ahead of me. Johnny was speaking from experience.

I nodded in agreement, but I couldn't say anything.

When I left for Houston on June 30th, Johnny sent me a picture he'd taken of my daughter when we were together. He'd written below it, "Remember your 'why'."

I held onto the picture because Johnny was right. We all need a why. And as for me, my family was mine.

I thought I was going into a good situation in Houston, but it didn't take long to realize it wasn't. I needed a team to believe in me, but sometimes you don't get that support as an undrafted player. They don't have to wait and see. They want what they pay for now and my injuries held me back. They cut me from the team after only four preseason games.

## JOHNN(IE)

The Cardinals picked me up off the waiver wire for the practice squad without having to work out for them. I loved being with the Cardinals because we lived in Arizona, and Viv's family was there. I was killing it! After our scrimmages, the receiver coach had me in the top five for performance. I was brought up from the practice squad to the active roster in week three or four. But during the first game, I pulled my hamstring and was placed on injured reserve (IR) for the rest of the year.

The following season, my ankle got banged up, making it challenging to practice, but I kept getting out there and giving it my all. After my knee injury, I didn't think anything could keep me from practicing or playing. That was the dog in me. I didn't want to be labeled as someone who didn't even want to practice. I wanted to be the person I became in college, not the one blaming my injuries. So, every day after practice, when someone saw my ankle all swollen, they'd ask me what happened, and I'd shrug it off as a temporary thing until my ankle got better. It's what I had to do. I'd put the boot on, which eased the pain and helped me feel more comfortable walking throughout the day. Some days it was just super sore, but as long as I could make it through the day, I wasn't trippin'.

As a result, I never had the chance to fully showcase my talent, which didn't help me stay in the league. Initially, they told one of the trainers they were planning to put me on injured reserve, so I thought they would keep me around. I think the coaches liked me, but they weren't fully invested in me because of my injuries, so they called me in and asked for my playbook.

My agent told me not to do anything so my ankle could heal. When I got the boot off, my ankle felt better. I had a five-day workout with the Jets, but I still couldn't perform the way I wanted. After that workout, the Giants picked me up and I performed well, but they didn't like the way the MRI of my ankle looked. They also had a knee clause in everything. If something happened to my knee, they didn't have to take care of it.

I continued working out for other teams, like Tampa Bay, waiting to be picked up by another team. This was in the middle of 2020 during COVID, so the workouts turned into a five-day ordeal, since we had to be tested first and cleared before we were able to get out on the field.

In 2021, I went back to Ohio State for Pro-Day and ran routes, then got picked up not long after that by Dallas. I attended the organized team activities (OTAs), went home for a little break, then back to camp. I played the next four preseason games—until I got cut again.

I found the depression coming back. I would walk around feeling angry. Although I didn't tell Viv about my depression, since we were living together, she couldn't help but notice how things were affecting me. Viv was strong. Without judgment, she pushed me to move past being released. She understood what football meant to me. Viv knew that I wasn't okay with not playing. It was painful. Incredibly painful, and that pain and darkness began to settle in. I'd sit and play Madden because at the time, that was all I thought or felt I could do. But because of Viv staying on me, my agent constantly trying to find opportunities, and my passion for the game, I didn't stay in that space long. I took every chance I got and kept trying out. I wasn't giving up.

I followed up with two workouts with the Colts. It was frustrating because my knees were working fine, but they were worried about the *future* of my knees and didn't sign me. Parris was hot! Drafted by the Colts, he thought we had a reasonable chance of playing together. The problem was that I didn't know if every team would have the same perspective, more concerned about my knees than what I could bring to the game. My career could have ended here, but I couldn't accept it. When I thought of Mama, Viv, and my daughter Zya, Johnny was right; I had to see it through for them.

In April of 2021, Viv and I had a son, Johnnie Lee Dixon IV—beautiful and perfect like his older sister. It was yet another reason to keep fighting for my dreams. I wanted to set a good example for him, too.

Getting past being released from the Cardinals set me up for that stage of reality coming at some point, but until then, I was stubborn and still working for the opportunity to play in the NFL.

# JOHNN(IE)

## FORGE • AHEAD

**WE DIDN'T KNOW IT** *at the time, but us forging a knife together was creating a lifelong friendship and a path that only God could have placed us on. We were sharpening each other through the difficulties we faced in life. These challenges were complex, but they allowed us to grow and become stronger through our conversations. We were each given raw materials—our experiences, talents, and strengths that were being shaped and molded into something beautiful and useful.*

*Forging a knife involves a series of steps that require patience, resilience, and focus. Johnny and I both saw parallels between the process of forging a knife and cultivating mental fortitude. We can all gain valuable insights into developing inner strength and mental resilience using the following steps:*

- **PREPARATION**: *Just as forging requires selecting the right materials and preparing the workspace,* building mental fortitude starts with setting clear goals, identifying challenges, and preparing oneself mentally for the journey ahead.

- **HEAT AND PRESSURE**: In the forging process, metal is heated to high temperatures and subjected to intense pressure to shape the steel into a blade. Similarly, developing mental fortitude to conquer your Goliath often involves facing adversity, discomfort, and situations under pressure that test one's resilience and determination.

- **PRECISION AND FOCUS**: Forging a knife requires precision and focus to shape the metal into the desired form. Similarly, cultivating mental fortitude involves honing one's focus, concentration, and attention to detail to navigate challenges and overcome obstacles effectively.

- **PATIENCE AND PERSEVERANCE**: The forging process is time-consuming and requires patience to achieve the desired results. Building mental fortitude requires patience and perseverance to stay committed to one's goals, even in the face of setbacks or slow progress.

- **REFINEMENT**: *Finally, the finished knife undergoes polishing and sharpening to refine its edges and improve its performance. Similarly, individuals can continue to refine and strengthen their mental fortitude through self-reflection, personal growth, and ongoing learning and development.*

*By drawing inspiration from the process of forging a knife, individuals can cultivate the qualities of patience, resilience, focus, and determination—all of which are needed to develop mental fortitude and navigate life's challenges with strength and grace.*

*God, thank you.*

# FORGE(D)

# roost(er)

## JOHNN(Y)

**WHEN IT CAME TO** the Marines, anyone who complained about everything and brought morale down was dangerous. And if we didn't trust someone, we wouldn't want to be around them. The Marines I'm referring to didn't want to work out, train, or get better. We couldn't motivate them to want to pick up their own lives because they just did not care, and it was tough. In Kuwait, I was promoted to Lance Corporal and then Corporal on my second tour. When it came to leadership and my team, I took it upon myself to demonstrate the leader-leader model. If I was the leader, I should lead people to aspire to be better, which is how we operated.

Some people I tried to lead couldn't get over the idea that they *could* die. They were more fixated on their fear of dying than their reasons to live. The level of mental fortitude needed for a constant real-life version of Russian Roulette is not something that every person is able to naturally acquire. But some people didn't even have a clear vision of what they were fighting for. That's why I'm such a believer in the power of the index card and making sure our whys are greater than our fears. It hurts to know that some people never lived long enough to figure out their why for risking their lives in the first place.

They all made the ultimate sacrifice. And to be clear, anyone who died gave their lives for our freedoms; they're my heroes. I don't care what they did before. Anyone killed made the ultimate sacrifice.

Two things that matter are who we become in life and what we give back to life.

I had Post-Traumatic Stress Disorder (PTSD) in the Marine Corps, and I didn't know it at the time. I don't know who does. In Iraq, I listened to music all the time. It was a source of motivation that helped keep my head in the right place. It wasn't until I came home between deployments that I noticed PTSD, which evolved from there. I had a lot of regret and anxiety in certain situations and carried a lot of unhealthy emotions.

If I saw a bag of trash or something on the side of the road, I didn't know if an IED was in it. I'd have anxiety or a panic attack, and I had to work through it. It didn't matter where I was; I was always on high alert. I guess you could say my senses were heightened—they still are. When I came home, a door slamming or any loud noise would startle me, and I'd jump. Whistling caused pretty high anxiety because we were always getting mortared, and that's a sound you don't forget. Large crowds were another trigger. Hell, after Iraq, the war became us versus ourselves. It's all shoved inside, and it travels everywhere I go.

Before PTSD started taking shape in darker and more destructive ways, I honestly thought I was just a badass Marine, then I realized I didn't care or give a crap about anything. It seemed like I got into a bar fight every other weekend and broke someone's jaw because I could. That's who I was. My guys and I have been in plenty of fights at parties. Sometimes, three of my guys and I would get into a bar fight. We'd knock out several guys and then leave. That's how we were, and hell no, that wasn't normal! Looking back on it, that was probably a component of PTSD. PTSD is extremely prevalent among military personnel deployed to Iraq and Afghanistan. For Marines, it's one of the most common mental health disorders.

Mental health is even harder when we come home, and we routinely have guys committing suicide. Routinely.

Their name gets posted in our 2/7 Facebook Group. In fact, we were told that our unit 2/7 currently has the highest suicide rate compared to any unit, any branch, within any war in history. We've lost more guys to suicide than we ever did in combat, validating why we say, "Only the dead see the end of war."

Following our return home from the first deployment I advocated for speaking up, especially if something didn't feel right. Between deployments, we had a new lieutenant who continually tried to make us do unnecessary training exercises that he most likely read in a book while in college. I'd seen the results of poor leadership and was afraid he was setting us up for failure. The lieutenant wanted us to learn how to use our entrenching tool, also known as an E-tool, as a grappling tool. With 550 cord, we would use it to drag concertina wire to us as we slowly crawled, then we'd cut the wire.

He wanted to simulate that we were infiltrating an enemy base. I spoke up saying it was a waste of time, as Iraqis and insurgents do not have bases in Iraq and we would never need to do this where we were going. The lieutenant became mad and stormed off, telling me to dismiss my squad back to the barracks. About an hour after the argument with the lieutenant, our Company Commander created a company formation. He ordered me to the front.

"If your Golden Boy is going to argue and be insubordinate, let this be an example for all of you. Dawson! You are now in Headquarters Platoon and removed from your Squad Leader position." *Golden Boy?* That was the first time I had ever heard that phrase and wasn't quite sure what it meant. I felt defeated at that moment. I was angered because I knew what I was doing was right, but at the same time, maybe I should have just allowed the lieutenant to conduct his useless exercise. I could not believe they called for a company formation just to kick me out of the platoon for insubordination.

The company Gunnery Sergeant called me to his office where I met with the Company Commander, Gunnery Sergeant, and First Sergeant, and they asked me what the hell happened. I explained that the LT was wasting valuable time and resources conducting a breaching exercise on concertina wire when we should be teaching the newer Marines how to identify IEDs, properly set up defensive positions, and care for the wounded. After explaining to my superiors the facts of what had occurred, they called in the LT and chewed him out pretty good while I waited in the hall. They reinforced to the LT that he was lucky to have me in the platoon looking out for his men and suggested that he take my advice if it were given. I was then placed back in my role as a Squad Leader within the platoon. This confirmed my concern about leadership, making me more vigilant moving forward.

Unfortunately, as fate would have it, I got injured during training, which affected my career. In 2005 we were preparing to go back to Fallujah, and I was doing a training maneuver where I dove to get behind cover and hit my hip on a rock. It hurt like hell, but I managed to push through until we went out on a Physical Fitness Test run. My hip popped, my leg locked up, and I fell over. When I got checked out, the doctor said I couldn't deploy because I tore my left hip labrum. They held me back to do physical therapy to strengthen my hip. Watching my whole squad go off to war without me was the hardest thing I had done in my life. I had grown-ass Marines bawling their eyes out getting on the bus to go to Iraq, while I watched and cried along with them. I was devastated that I couldn't go with them because of my hip injury. That messed me up.

I drank and slept with women left and right, ran from the police—I was a mess. I was someone I never wanted to be. Then I heard that one of my guys, Caffarelli, was shot in the head. He turned his head to look at another guy, and at that exact moment, a sniper shot him in his Kevlar, which saved his life. That hit me, and I wished I could have been there, but I wasn't.

Knowing they were all going through that without me tore me apart. Feeling helpless, I told them that staying here wasn't doing me any good, and I started asking every single unit to send me back. I went to my command and said, "I don't care who's going over next. I'm going."

Colonel Crowe, 1st Marine Division Regimental Combat Team 7 were the next on deck to return. I was one of just a few guys with prior combat experience. I volunteered to go and was assigned as Gunner White's personal protector. I was both the Vehicle Commander of his 50-caliber armored vehicle and personal 50-caliber machine gun gunner. Gunner White worked within the regiment with Colonel Crowe. Unfortunately, they weren't leaving until January, so I returned home on leave.

I wanted to spend time with my grandma before I left. She was getting older, and her health was getting worse. And even though I always told my guys never to get married before deployment, I met someone before I left for Iraq for my second deployment, who I later ended up eloping with.

I told Mom and my stepdad I was returning to Iraq, and they understood. I knew it wasn't what Mom wanted to hear when I told her I had volunteered to return, especially since she went through some challenging times during my first tour overseas. It wasn't like I could pick up a cell phone and call her. Sometimes I was out on operations for three or four weeks, and she didn't know if I was dead or alive. I'd been on the phone with her while we were getting mortared and attacked back in Hit. I would run out to help while she was left on the other end of the phone, waiting for me to return.

As much as I love my mother, I felt needed over there. Not back here. And the lives of my men were more important than my own.

When I returned to Iraq with the Colonel, I only saw my old platoon because they were coming out of Iraq as I was going in. It felt like a dig at me because I got hurt and wasn't there when all that shit happened. I felt like I had let my platoon down.

I had a whole new squad that I had to train up and get ready. They put this platoon together as security for the Colonel and only four of us out of 30 were Marines with infantry combat experience. Everyone else fell into the category of POGs, "people other than grunts," usually welders, cooks, electricians, and communications. From Kuwait to Iraq, we had to teach them how to be like us. I loved that they didn't have any egos.

263

They listened, adapted, took orders well, and became a fighting force. It worked out.

On my last deployment, I met a guy named Mike who worked for the Colonel I was protecting. This was my second deployment, and everyone knew I'd been to combat, so I was on the varsity team. Everyone else was JV. Just to lighten the mood, I made fun of all the officers. Mike was a nerdy Marine with big glasses. He wasn't afraid of combat; he always wanted to go with us, but we told him no because he'd get himself or one of us killed. That probably wasn't true, but that's what we told him to try and keep him on base.

Mike was a reservist from Texas. I asked him what he did, and he told me. I had no idea that financial services existed as a career. The most I knew about stocks was the project I did in school. When it came to wealth, *Rich Dad Poor Dad* was it; yet my interest was surprisingly strong. Mike explained that he helped people plan for retirement, invest in stocks, and make other financial decisions. I made a deal with Mike that he could train me on Sundays if I wasn't going outside the wire.

Mike opened a class for anyone interested, but I was the only one who showed up. I learned more from Mike than anyone could imagine, which is the reason I was able to purchase my first house. He helped me open a Roth IRA and a brokerage account. I didn't waste my combat pay. Instead, I invested in it in 2006. My basic pay was about $1,842/month as an E-4 with an additional $225/month for "imminent danger" or "hostile fire" pay.

The Colonel's security team had a year's deployment; we were supposed to be with him for the duration he was there, but I reinjured my hip nine months later. We had a few long foot patrols to set up on IED hot spots and I tore my labrum even more because of the weight of the packs. Sitting in a Humvee with the weight of the flak jacket caused excruciating pain in my hip.

Upon returning home to have hip surgery, I informed the doctor about the persistent aching in my wrist. It had been hurting me for some time. We had an IED explode in between our Humvees while on a routine patrol in which I jammed my wrist on the radio console. I'm glad their timing was off that day; I'd been taping it so I could go outside the wire. The doctors said it appeared that I broke my wrist, so they had to break and reset it, then place some pins in my wrist to strengthen it. After two surgeries in the same month, I was in bed for six to eight weeks, unable to do anything. Next, I had physical therapy for another eight months.

During that time, I took an advanced paramedic course through Copper Mountain College and became an EMT, in the hopes that I would have more knowledge when I returned to the Middle East. Although I took physical therapy seriously, I found out that I couldn't go back, and even if I re-enlisted, the Marine Corps wouldn't allow me to remain in a combat unit due to my injuries.

That was pretty much the end of my military career. June 10th, 2007 marked the predestined conclusion of my time within the Marine Corps, as my period of service reached its natural end. I chose not to reenlist. The decision stemmed from the restriction from serving within a combat unit due to my hip injury. That meant I wouldn't be with my men.

I didn't handle it well. It was a challenge both mentally and physically. No matter how hard I tried, the

## JOHNN(Y)

Marine Corps would always remain a part of me. Surprisingly, what was harder was returning to a world where "war" isn't something you can just put down on a résumé and obtain a respectable job. My next mission was going to Ohio State to better myself and get an education.

When I got back, I didn't show any joy or love for anyone, not even my spouse at the time, because I hated everything, and I spiraled from there. I'd wake up, see my Marines' faces, and hear their voices like it just happened yesterday.

The flashbacks became more intense once I was home. They're caused by combat stressors that remind me of traumatic situations. Triggers. Loud noises. Smells. Something that's out of place. It could be anything related to the trauma I experienced, but an example would be the whistle of a mortar or being near an exploding IED.

We were driving down a supply route in our Humvee, and suddenly saw the brightest white flash you can imagine. That IED makes the loudest sound on the planet. After that, you're in a daze. The first thing that happens is the world slows down, everything seems to be in slow motion and you instantly begin to wonder if you or any of your men are injured. It's a confusing state of mind, but you have to react quickly.

The PTSD from IED explosions was severe enough to cause night terrors because I still have them. Veterans or anyone who has experienced some form of trauma might live with PTSD. We're not crazy. We're traumatized.

One of my old platoon Sergeants, Jon Brodin, also known as T-1000, and I spotted a pressure plate IED. The enemy would take IV tubing or some type of tube, put wires inside of it and lay it across the road. If the wires touched, it exploded. The Humvees in front of us passed it, but I was in the last Humvee, and I saw it as we passed it. We'd usually drive down the middle of the road, but we were lucky they didn't stick it out far enough to reach our tires. We barely missed running over it!

The standard procedure whenever we found an IED was to call Explosive Ordinance Disposal (EOD). It could take four to 12 hours for them to come out and blow it up, and we had to sit there and wait for those guys. Staff Sergeant Brodin was with us, and this guy was on our first deployment. He'd been in multiple combat situations before Iraq: Somalia, the Gulf War. This guy had been in the Marine Corps for a long time, and everyone followed his lead. In our unit he was legendary, and a big reason I volunteered to go back was that I knew I was going with him. In the middle of talking about the IED, he said, "Let's look at it!"

I recalled what happened during my first deployment to the three guys who jumped in the hole with an IED. "I'm not going to look at it."

"You won't look at it with me?" This translated to: *You won't go die with me if I blow us up?*

I conceded, which illustrates I was always ready to die. It was like roulette, an adrenaline rush with no other comparison.

We walked up to the IED, with the wire sticking out of a small mound of dirt rising from the ground. I stood, peering over his shoulder as if his body would somehow save me, even though I knew that was a lie. Brodin just reached down, grabbed the wire, and ripped it from the ground!

"I guess we don't need EOD to come out now!"

Those memories, when they're triggered, cause PTSD. My nightmares are of that exact moment, but it always explodes. It's pretty scary. Maybe now you can understand why I said I was always ready to die. That was just one of many situations where I felt I would die.

Imagine having a nightmare about an event that has left a deep scar on your psyche. Now, think about that nightmare replaying, not just when you sleep but unpredictably when you're awake. When PTSD is triggered, it's like a replay button was hit, bringing back the terrifying moment with startling clarity. It feels so immediate that it's almost as if the event is occurring all over again.

PTSD isn't just about having bad memories. It's about living with a mind that can't let go of those terrifying moments and continues to replay them, making life a relentless cycle of anxiety, fear, and distress. It's hell.

Some of the most significant battles weren't overseas. They were at home. I was in the darkest place I'd ever been, and it contributed to one of several factors that ended my marriage. There were too many bad memories, images, and night terrors from Iraq. No one should carry that kind of pain. Jon, Mohammad, Vicente, and guys getting blown up until there's nothing left to send home isn't normal; no matter how much the Marines desensitized or rebuilt us, it's not easy to process or forget. There was a lot of death, and with it came pain and sadness. I still had responsibilities, so I just held everything I felt inside until I didn't feel I could anymore.

I've had some unbearable moments and one night it all came to a head. After drinking pretty heavily and playing Call of Duty, I went upstairs to my room, blasted "Rooster" by Alice In Chains, then dumped the nightstand drawer on the floor. I grabbed my gun, feeling the cold of the Glock pistol grip in my hand as I sat on the edge of the bed. Tears started slowly streaming down my face and I saw the flashes of the last few moments of my life as I closed my eyes, lifting the pistol to my mouth.

Rocky began whimpering, placing his head in my lap. As I opened my eyes to what I believed was one last time, I looked down at my big-eared German Shepherd, Rocky, and beside him on the floor was my index card, the FEAR side of my card facing up showing my number one FEAR, death. I thought, *if I'm dead, sitting in a pool of blood, what would this dog do? Did David, Jon, Hendu, and Mohammad all die for nothing if I'm about to pull this trigger? I'm leaving my best friend, my only friend, which is a dog.*

For whatever reason, Rocky wouldn't leave me alone. My eyes welled with tears that wouldn't stop falling. Rocky was whining and relentlessly licking my face. I swear he wouldn't stop, like he knew what I was about to do and was trying to stop me. I couldn't do it and I chose at that moment to focus on my whys in this life instead as the music blared, *"no, no, no, you know he ain't gonna die!"*

My ex was only supposed to let me have Rocky for that weekend as she took him initially when we split up. However, following that night and now knowing Rocky was not only my best friend, but my protector, I told her she was never getting him back.

Most people don't know what triggers PTSD, the exact cause of depression or deep-seated pain until it manifests in the form of anger or suicidal ideation. I was very adept at internalizing trauma, too, until I wasn't. When it comes to mental health—sometimes with us veterans, the war inside becomes too intense, and unless you're a veteran, it can be difficult to understand.

The Veterans Affairs Vocational Rehabilitation Program recommended that I meet with a psychologist or a therapist. I went to one meeting, but when I walked into the office and saw the therapist was a Middle Eastern man, I said, "No offense. I don't feel comfortable having a meeting with you," and left. When I walked into his office, the smell of Middle Eastern scents hit me, and I just shut down. In time, I understood that everything I went through was the suffering I had to endure to change the outcome of my life. And if it weren't for that mustard seed of faith I had somewhere inside of me, I would have committed suicide.

PTSD is like drug and alcohol addiction. It's a daily proactive battle to have the mental fortitude to believe the past is the past and that I don't have to allow the past to determine my circumstances in life. The story of David and Goliath in the Bible is the best story for PTSD. People don't realize that once David defeated Goliath, he was put in every single conflict or war. In Psalm 55, David is contemplating suicide, but by the end of the chapter, he gives the burden to God and asks him to take the enemy's voices away, let him live in peace, and God did that for me.

However, even knowing what I know now, I'd enlist again if it meant I could join my brothers in combat. I'd do it a hundred times over. Unfortunately, many people aren't mentally strong enough to protect our country and go through things like that or do it successfully. This is still the greatest nation on the planet. And because of our military, almost anyone can come to this country and build a life of their virtue and value. It takes men and women with a selfless mentality to protect the freedoms we enjoy in this country. To be a part of that is one of the greatest gifts I've ever received.

# JOHNN(Y)

# FORGE • AHEAD

**SITTING ON THE EDGE** of the bed, holding a pistol while Rocky was at my feet, I listened to "Rooster" by Alice In Chains, a song I heard a thousand times. It wasn't until then that I understood the depths of its meaning. The song was written by guitarist Jerry Cantrell. He wrote it about his father, a Vietnam veteran, whom he resented at an early age due to the struggles he had with PTSD. Jerry never understood his father's PTSD struggles and wrote the song from the lens of his perspective, which mirrored mine after Iraq. Regardless of how often I thought I'd die, I didn't. They could never "snuff the Rooster." However, in my darkest moments, war stole the ability to reason and understand that I was given a greater purpose.

Ironically, "Rooster" by Alice In Chains became a song I often listened to through my struggles. I saw them live at Rock on the Range one year in Columbus. My buddy Joel and I made our way to the front, and once "Rooster" played,

I was flooded with emotion from Iraq and remembering the night I almost ended my life. I broke down and cried as Joel tried to console me in the middle of thousands of people.

In the Holler, roosters had a deeper meaning. Typically, they were the first thing we heard, signaling the start of a new day. However, if I'd taken my life listening to the very symbol that sounded a new day from my earlier years, I would have given up the ability to hear the crow and change my path.

Like a rooster crowing as the sun peaked across the Appalachian pines, listening to Alice In Chains served as a mental alarm clock. It helped me begin again with a clear and focused mindset. Our thoughts can often become too loud and unsettling. Emotions can become too overwhelming or unhealthy if we allow them to dominate our minds and behaviors, just as I did several years after leaving the war.

Today, what type of crow do you hear from your own rooster? Is it loud and too frequent, or do you understand that the crow reminds you of a new day filled with hope and purpose? Try to manage your thoughts and emotions by practicing self-care, seeking support from those you trust or professionals, and engaging in healthy activities. Listen to your rooster!

Rocky, thank you.

# ROOST(ER)

# scar(s)

## JOHNN(IE)

**WHEN A PROBLEM IS** bigger than us or our capability to handle it, we need something or someone bigger than us to help. It isn't a sign of weakness. It's a sign you want to be whole, a sign of strength. Communicating what we need to get out helps. I love football, but the stress of not playing was depressing. I loved being at Ohio State, but losing family and friends while away at college was painful and caused tremendous guilt. I had the goal of playing in the NFL, but my injuries threatened to kill my dream and keep me from getting Mama into a better home. And although my thoughts were self-imposed, as her oldest child, I felt that was my responsibility, especially given how she supported me. All of these things combined were too much for me to process. Things affect us when we don't expect them to. If we did, we'd be better prepared. It just hit me. *I'm human.*

Many people have depression for several reasons, and it holds them back from the next level, whether in sports, their career, or life. Depression can stem from what's supposed to be positive experiences or moments, when what we love isn't working. If something doesn't feel right, it's not. There were days I was alright. I'm a jolly guy. I love to laugh, but other days I just needed to talk and get my frustrations out so I could get back to being me.

I, for damn sure, didn't like being stuck under a blanket with the dark emotions I was going through. When you hit that point, even if you're typically a private individual that keeps things to yourself, drop your shoulders, take a deep breath, and spill the beans! Get it out. Talking about it was cool, and I wish I did it sooner.

When you interview and choose the right therapist, there's no judgment. Your feelings are validated, and you can work toward solutions. I think it's healthy to get things off your chest. And if we have a mental barrier, we won't overcome it until we let someone in who can help. We're all fighting the same battle and are more alike than we care to believe.

Pain, trauma, death, and anxiety have the same value to some. Still, there are a lot of people with mental health issues who respond differently to adverse situations and spiral. My point is it's common. Too common. There's no one way for things to hit people, and there's not one demographic that it misses. I went to therapy when I felt something was wrong and found out I was dealing with depression. I didn't tell Mama or Viv because I didn't want to worry them. I already had a staunch support team from Ohio State. But I had to take action, one foot in front of the other, to get the help I needed to get over the depression.

I knew my journey, but when we look into the eyes of another man or human being, even if they tell us, we don't know the depths or the entirety of their story. We didn't feel it, live it, or walk even a quarter mile in their shoes at their lowest or most challenging point. We can only listen and care enough to learn from one another without judgment. We don't exactly know what they've endured or why, but we can treat one another better, kinder.

I enjoy being around people, creating new experiences, learning who they are and what made them that way. And I also understand that whatever our history is, it contributes to who we become. Turning the pages helps bring a greater understanding of others. Doing things with people who are different closes the gap.

Football set the standard for me. Players come from all over the country with dissimilar backgrounds, cultures, races, upbringings, economic statuses, political perspectives, and beliefs. But somehow, our coaches are experts at bringing all of those differences together and making them work successfully. They teach and encourage us to respect one another at the highest level so we can achieve the goal of being a great team—as one. We train and then play our games as a team with one goal. If we don't, we won't be successful. The bottom line is that we're stronger together, not independently.

If we can navigate our differences and find success as a team, why can't the rest of the world do it? Some are afraid or hate too deeply to do that. However, my response is that maybe you won't ever get to see the full experience of yourself if you don't take those uncomfortable leaps.

I've learned to take the time to look deeper into someone and discover who they really are before judging a book by its cover. Most often, when people get to know you, you're different from what they think. Just like people, the cover of a book doesn't reveal the full story. But I try to get in-depth on those pages and go through the chapters to find out more. We won't fully understand someone unless we sit down with them as our authentic selves without wanting or needing anything from them.

Pick the brains of those you love and new people you meet; determine how they move and think, and most importantly, pay attention to how they treat others. I have great conversations with people who look like me and who don't. I'm sure football helped with that. It made it easy for people to have something in common with me, but we need to do that in other areas of our lives. I love cooking and photography, and there's so much more that people would identify with if they took the time to get to know me.

When I was going through my struggles physically and mentally, as the dreams I worked for my entire life slipped through my hands, I was discouraged for a second, but God kept trying to tell me I had other gifts to explore and nurture. Maybe football was the platform to help me do more, but I gotta see it through. I think my purpose is bigger, and it's something I've been questioning and battling through my injuries. But it's a part of the journey and a part of the story.

God is trying to help me place my hands on something. I definitely questioned what I was doing so wrong, but I never stopped praying. I'd sit in the middle of practice, close my eyes, and pray. Stuff got hard, but I knew He's always been there, and He was still there. God has given me so much that I couldn't give up on believing. There's a greater good to my story.

Although I didn't play in many games, I take pride in having made it to the NFL. What I've learned is that good or bad, I appreciate my life's experiences because of the man they've made me. It gave me a more resilient mindset, the most significant benefit of overcoming hurdles and obstacles, even if it means asking for help to work through adversity.

Friends like Johnny kept me going through the tough times. They uplifted me, kept me pushing forward and connected, and constantly filled me with positivity even when they didn't know I needed it. Hell, I didn't know how badly I needed it.

People say they're self-made, but I'm always reminding them, "You're never self-made. You've never done anything in this life by yourself. You've always had a team of coaches, teachers, mentors, your network, church, co-workers, or people inspiring or helping in some way." Having a supportive team around you is one of the best things in life.

It's easy for others to bring morale down. If one of our teammates wasn't on the same standard, he probably wasn't lining up next to you on the field on game day. Our coach had a strategy. He'd put those guys next to the leaders during summer workouts, intentionally pairing us with someone who didn't work as hard as we did. When the younger guys came in, our job was to get them up to speed and meet the program's standards.

If the team wasn't on the same page regarding dedication and work ethic, it could translate to loss of games. This strategy was meant to ensure that the team had a sense of unity and that everyone worked equally hard. By having the leaders and more experienced players work alongside the younger players, they could help guide them and set an example of the standards that the team expected. This created a culture of hard work and dedication, ensuring that the team would be able to perform at its optimal level and win games.

You can't lose one game when you're on a level like Ohio State. There are too many good teams in that division. We're not playing for a record—we're playing for a national title! Elite coaches, like ours, can pull teams together while others remain divided.

That's effective leadership. A chain is only as strong as its weakest link. If the chain has a crack, eventually that chain will break. But, if you come together and strengthen that link, then the whole chain will be stronger. We're always stronger together than we are individually.

It was killing me when I couldn't play with my team because I gave them everything I had. My whole life, I gave football everything. I was terrified that my injury would end my career and I avoided that fear as much as I could. But the thing that scares you is usually the thing that develops you.

Bottom line, I wanted to do what I went to O State to do, and sitting around injured wasn't it. My deepest fear came true when my injuries put an end to my dream of playing in the NFL, but the process that I've been through, while it has taken from me, it's made me a better man. I don't think any of us understand how we're changing and growing from moment to moment. You only see your growth in hindsight.

For many, childhood can be a battlefield with deep-seated traumas and profound pain. While I didn't grow up with every luxury, I always had enough. Enveloped in love and support, nurtured in a spiritual bond with God, I received everything I needed. My heart overflowed with genuine gratitude and joy. I came to know my family, and they were always there, their presence a comforting constant. We were interconnected in a chain of mutual support and that meant everything—if one of us lacked something, the others were there to fill the gap. When my mother needed time for herself, my aunt was always ready to step in.

Despite the unshakeable bond I shared with my family and friends, the realities of growing up in the hood fueled my motivation to seek other opportunities and other ways of life. This isn't to say I'd never sever ties with my roots; rather, it sparked an insatiable hunger for more. Everyone who made it out pushed themselves to be better. They didn't want to go back. Though Mama never complained about her life, I was driven to change that for her.

Watching Mama and my grandmother, I know I was built to be resilient. Mama worked two jobs, and my grandmother was so different in the way she thought. Her "I don't give a f—k about anything" meter was through the roof! Mama, Auntie Tevia, and Auntie Shirley were the same way. I was around strong women. I watched them push through difficult situations, observing how they operated throughout my life. They made me decide whether I'd be like them or someone else.

I wasn't always mentally tough. That was cultivated over time through experiences and my environment.

Unfortunately, mental toughness can deteriorate in the same way. Growing up, not everyone around me reached the level they wanted, but some never gave up. They continued to push through. I almost gave in when I quit football. However, I had to move past the mental piece because I didn't intend to fail. I didn't want kids coming behind me to see me fail and think that success was an unconquerable giant. That we couldn't get out and stay out. I saw Devin Hester make it out of the hood so there's no reason I couldn't. The hood was a driving factor because I knew I'd be stuck if I didn't make it out.

I didn't want anyone to think it was hopeless if I didn't make it.

Being committed to football made me more dedicated, disciplined, and faithful as a man, son, husband, father, friend, brother, and child of God. Football has given me a platform that helped me see that I can accomplish whatever I believe I can. That's how I made it, the same as those before me.

I've played football my whole life. I was good, and I loved it, but when you're a ball player, you miss a lot of other things. I've found that I'm not as confident outside of football yet, but I'm working to eliminate that lack of confidence. Football became more of my identity than I would have thought. When I have that helmet and uniform on, I am a different person than I am without it. It's not the same. Still, we have to keep going and figure life out. It's worth it.

So, I continued moving forward with my life. I entered the USFL draft and was the second receiver drafted by the New Orleans Breakers. It was my first year and I didn't have any expectations, but my teammates made it fun, and I enjoyed it. I collected a few more memories. As for my future, it's taking a very different shape. I'm at peace because I don't want to keep putting my eggs in that basket, and I think it's a wise decision to move on and pursue other things. Football won't be my only narrative forever. At some point, I will have to pivot.

While I've committed to playing a second season in the USFL, I view it as a transition one way or the other, but my passion is still strong. In the meantime, Johnny and I are working together to help people understand mental health and its importance, and how to get support.

## JOHNN(IE)

I've found that life has a habit of leaving marks on us. Some are visible, others hidden. Each one of these is a testament to a unique struggle, a singular trial that we've overcome. The scars etched on my knees, for instance, are enduring reminders of pain, fear, uncertainty, and the adversities that my injuries precipitated.

While we all bear scars—some from physical battles, others from mental or emotional tribulations, the way we perceive these marks can significantly shape our outlook on life. And it's different for everyone.

We're all in this life together and the best thing we can do is help each other. It starts with taking the time to get to know each other.

# SCAR(S)

## FORGE • AHEAD

**TODAY, I SEE MY** *scars, but they're not painful reminders of my past. Instead, they're badges of honor—each marking adversity that attempted to divert me from my journey. The right support network, mental resilience, and relentless determination can transform these reminders of past struggles into potent symbols of personal growth, strength, and endurance, just as they have for me.*

*While my physical scars have mended, allowing me to reignite my fervor for football, I am acutely aware of the necessity to attend to the impressions that remain invisible to the naked eye. It is essential to appreciate the deeper significance of these scars, that they can often be caused by anxiety and depression and can leave a deeper impact on your life and outcome. If you carry any enduring scars—physical, psychological, or emotional—I implore you to cease hiding them. Instead, illuminate these imprints to those who sincerely have your best interest at heart and desire to see and help you flourish while leading a* meaningful life. One of my deepest invisible scars was battling depression. It was hiding under the surface during some of my darkest days. It was challenging to move on after depression; here are five steps that helped me:

- **GRADUAL TRANSITION**: Make small positive steps that can lead to significant improvements, allowing yourself time to adjust while ensuring sustainable progress.

- **SET NEW GOALS**: Create meaningful and realistic goals focusing on personal growth and experiences. Maybe this means going for a walk once a day or meeting up with a friend once a week.

- **BUILD A ROUTINE**: Create structure in your daily routine that includes activities you enjoy that can contribute to your overall health. Consistency can provide a sense of purpose and stability.

- **DEVELOP CONNECTIONS**: Strengthen the meaningful relationships in your life while spending time in prayer. Social connections can be vital in creating a positive environment and emotional support.

- **PROFESSIONAL FOLLOW-UP**: Continue your regular check-ins with mental health professionals and mentors. Discuss your progress and celebrate your accomplishments. Develop healthy strategies for maintaining good mental health.

After all, our scars are not just remembrances of past conflicts—they are emblems of our resilience, strength, and the Goliaths we've courageously triumphed over.

Viv, thank you.

# ultra(sound)

## JOHNN(Y)

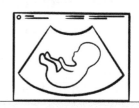

**MY JOURNEY BACK TO** my faith wasn't easy, but as God would have it—it was inevitable.

Though Borah wouldn't give me the time of day when I first met her, she held onto my number. A year later, she sent a text message asking if I was still living in Ohio, and our communication unfolded from there. When Borah and I started dating, I had tickets to go to New Orleans for the Sugar Bowl. I asked her if she could keep Rocky for the weekend and without hesitation, she said yes. But while I was in New Orleans, Borah called me hysterical because Rocky was barking and growling as she opened the door and wouldn't let her inside her apartment! I kid you not; he was an amazingly intelligent dog. When I returned from New Orleans, Borah and I began dating exclusively.

Borah had heard the term PTSD but didn't know what it meant until she witnessed it. She had an Android phone, and it had a setting she had activated where it would blink—the camera light would flash a few times on the back—when she received a notification. The first night she stayed at my house, her phone went off and flashed simultaneously. It was normal to her, but I panicked. Really panicked.

"Borah! You have to turn that off! You can't keep that!" I yelled.

"What do you mean? Why?" she asked. She had no idea the flash on her phone was a trigger. She grabbed her phone and shut it off.

"I literally thought it was an IED going off!" I tried to explain. I was in intense distress. I didn't sleep that night. There was incredible sadness, coupled with fear for something only visible to me that she didn't yet understand.

Concerned about what happened, she googled "how do you know if someone has post-traumatic stress disorder" and learned I had displayed nearly every

296

symptom at some point. She didn't know how badly it would affect my life or how angry I would be, unable to hold tightly to positive emotions.

As we approached the end of January 2011, during my senior year at Ohio State, Borah was expecting our first child. I struggled to reconcile with the reality of impending fatherhood. In an act of total transparency, I admitted to Borah that I wasn't prepared for this responsibility, mentally, emotionally, nor financially. My emotional scars ran so deep that when I was faced with the affection of this radiant, spiritual woman, I was at a loss for how to respond.

Considering all of the things Borah wasn't aware of, it didn't take long for her to access the entirety of the situation. She was living with someone who was unpredictable, with emotional triggers that caused mood swings and sudden waves of pain and grief that I tried to suppress with alcohol. I didn't talk about Iraq with Borah. I didn't talk about death. I didn't want her to know what I'd seen or what was devouring the inside of me, but it was coming out in the worst ways. You can't hide PTSD. What I was putting her through was too much for anyone.

The look in her beautiful eyes said it all and made me question our relationship. I wasn't made for anything but war, and Borah saw a sliver through a crack in the door to my soul. The pain was forcing its way out, and I was afraid of what would happen when it did.

I had a lot of friends and drinking buddies. When Borah and I met, I was constantly hanging out with them. She tried to talk to me about it, but I wouldn't accept anything she said, as if she couldn't possibly understand. She eventually came to realize I existed in a world that only my brothers in Iraq understood. She imagined most of them were probably dealing with it the same way, or worse. It took a long time before I would open up. She didn't know how to support me at that time, which made her feel helpless. I didn't want her to see what I physically and mentally survived, and how it threatened to destroy me.

Compounded with having PTSD and depression, I was drinking way too much, and had nothing but unhealthy relationships behind me. All of this left me nowhere near whole and without faith. I needed to work on myself, and I hadn't yet begun. Everything changed the day Borah called with a request.

"I have an appointment for an ultrasound to hear the baby's heartbeat. Will you go?" I agreed, and even Mom came along. When I heard his delicate heartbeat, I fell in love with him. That calling wasn't the only one I'd have. I felt the Holy Spirit calling me again. This time, it was to do something more, using what I'd learned as a Marine. I told Borah I didn't know what I needed to do to figure out my stuff or what it would take to change, but I wanted to make it work. That was the first time Borah ever saw me cry; we both cried. Somehow, Borah knew what it would take, so she gave me an ultimatum.

"Johnny, I wasn't raised in a faith-based home. Faith wasn't talked about. And our relationship is volatile because of your drinking, which isn't going to get rid of your suffering. I'm working through things and I'm on a journey to find my faith. Johnny, I know if we don't put God first, it isn't going to work." Borah insisted. "And you can't derail me from what I'm doing. So the deal is, if we're going to make this work, you have to come to church with me on Sundays."

# ULTRA(SOUND)

Trying to shove my pain, issues, and hardness aside, I thought if that's what she needed from me to make us work, I'd do it. Apparently, Borah knew her demand was more significant than I did; it was probably the only thing that could make us, and my life, work for the better. But first, I had to build a better foundation to take care of my family in a much healthier way, and that foundation was me.

Besides attending Midnight Mass with my buddy Titus, I kept my word and went to church with Borah for the first time since I was an adult. The sermon was about aligning your heart and mind, and mine wasn't. It forced me to look at myself and admit I had a heart problem. I lacked emotion and vulnerability. I lacked empathy and fostered resentment toward anyone who hadn't experienced combat. Here I was, listening to a sermon that focused on every one of my deficiencies, causing me to realize my problem was me—and everything I lacked prevented me from living and building a healthy life. There was a point that if I had a problem, mostly with loss, I began blaming someone else—leadership in the Marine Corps, everything and everyone around me, even God. Instead, what I needed to do with my problems was trust God and dive deep inside my heart to find the solution.

With faith, all things are possible. When we left the church, I told Borah, "I really feel like that sermon was directed at me." She nodded in agreement. That particular sermon removed the stone around my heart, and I felt it crumbling off, leaving me with a sense of joy and peace I never had. From that moment, I decided this woman, who loved me enough to reconnect my relationship with God, had my whole heart.

Wanting our relationship to work and to give our child a healthy home environment, in September, I moved her in. During her pregnancy, I was still in a place of growth, and although we weren't engaged or married, I tried to be what Borah deserved. Every Sunday, we attended church and participated in their activities. It wasn't long before I started volunteering. Borah helped with the daycare ministry.

The more involved with the sports ministry I became, I felt that it was helping cultivate my faith. I was serving others and felt rooted in scripture and the truth, trying to apply it to my life. The process was like planting a seed in the ground and watching it grow.

Borah and I were investing in our faith, which strengthened our relationship.

The more time I invested in the church and God, I saw and felt my relationship with Christ begin to grow and become stronger. In the most powerful way, it began liberating me from the negative emotions and resentments I harbored, allowing me to have a sense of peace in ways I'd never known. I concluded that God put me on this path and gave me a purpose. Even though I'd lost friends, and I was still losing friends, I was starting to realize that it wasn't for nothing, and I had to forgive myself.

In September 2011, I was working full-time at a printing press while taking classes full time. Knowing that Borah was the woman I wanted to spend the rest of my life with, I bought a ring and decided to propose. When Maddox Wayne was born, the nurses transported him to the warming station. Borah and I were in the best place we had ever been.

I walked into the hospital gift shop and purchased a baby bracelet. I placed Borah's engagement ring on the bracelet, then slipped it around Maddox's leg. I dropped to my knees after handing our son to Borah and proposed. Borah was beyond beautiful. Her essence, her soul, and her words inspired me to be my best. We didn't have everything figured out, but Borah was certain that the path was through my relationship with God. She loved me enough to start at the beginning. Still numb from the epidural and high on the drugs they gave her for delivery, it worked in my favor—Borah said, "Yes!"

Unfortunately, our relationship had other challenges. One of them was that I got laid off from the printing press the Tuesday before Christmas. It was my senior year at Ohio State and I didn't know how we'd manage, especially having a newborn. While I hadn't shared everything about my military career with Borah—the loss of life, what triggered my PTSD, the trauma, how deep my depression went, and my inability to feel the way healthy people could—intuitively she knew losing my job was one more thing weighing on me. I was devastated. Having a family and not having a paycheck to pay our bills was stressful.

Borah, who always looked at the positive side of things from such a beautiful lens inside her soul, attempted to, at least temporarily, remove stress and bring a sense of joy by suggesting that we open our Christmas gifts the day I lost my job. We stood firm with our favorite verse as Borah reminded me, "Jeremiah 29:11 says, 'For I know the plans I have for you,' declares the Lord, 'plans to prosper you and not to harm you, plans to give you hope and a future.' We will get through this."

A few months after losing my job, I needed to run to the store for a few items. When I left, I noticed Rocky was laying upstairs in the hallway and seemed a little off. While at the store, Borah called me saying that Rocky hadn't moved and wouldn't get up. I rushed home to find him lying in the exact spot as he was before, his stomach felt really bloated. I knew something was wrong.

I rushed him to Ohio State's Veterinary Hospital that evening. After several tests they asked Borah and me to join them in a tiny room. They explained that Rocky had a tumor attached to his kidney and other organs that ruptured and tested positive for cancer. I asked how we could help him, and they explained they could remove the tumor and begin chemo treatments, but it may only add another six months to a year to his life. Additionally, the cost would be approximately $7,000, in addition to the nearly $3,000 I'd already spent on the test and treatments he had received thus far.

I became emotional immediately and felt defeated. A newborn son, struggling relationship, lost my job, and now Rocky. Borah and I both cried and prayed for help. I didn't have the money to help him, and our only option was to give him a peaceful death as his standard of living would never be the same. Borah and I stood next to the bed where he laid on his side with IVs sticking out of his leg.

The doctor asked if we would like to have a minute alone with him. I knelt down and petted the fur in between his little paw, telling him how sorry I was and asking him to forgive me. We both knew he saved my life and here I was making the hard decision to take his. It was undoubtedly the most difficult night of my life. I could see the fear in his eyes as the doctors began to inject the medicine into his IV and I kissed him on his nose one last time, tears streaming down my face.

As his eyes began to close and I hugged him tightly, at that moment I knew Rocky had lived just long enough for me to find Borah. He knew that from that point forward she would help me overcome my mental challenges. After the holidays and Rocky passing, reality ensued, and I started doing everything I could to secure another job. I interviewed with the FBI and obtained an unpaid internship with the Secret Service, which allowed me to protect President Obama, Vice President Biden, and Governor Romney during the 2012 Election.

One morning, after Borah's recommendation, I drove to a job fair. I had spoken with several different companies when I spotted a major financial institution displaying a military banner. They were hiring veterans to become financial advisors. I immediately headed that way.

"Do I need a financial background to apply?" I asked.

The gentleman working at the booth said, "No." I began explaining that I was working on my degree in criminology, studying Arabic, and trying to get into law enforcement. Suddenly, his eyes widened.

His eyes darted to my name tag, and he asked, "Are you from Circleville?"

"Yeah."

"Did you enlist in the Marines?"

306

"I did."

"In what year?"

"2003." And suddenly, the pieces fell into place. This was the recruiter in charge of the station to which I had reported when I enlisted. He had since retired from the Marines and was now part of the financial company I was inquiring about.

"The pay is $18.00 an hour. You study from home and then take the Series 7 license exam."

"I'll get paid to study from home?"

"Correct. And you have three months to do it."

"Sign me up!"

I was proficient in studying and confident in my testing abilities. Having recently lost my job and my graduation looming in June, I knew I had to do whatever was necessary to support my family. Helping others with their finances couldn't be more demanding than the challenges I'd already faced. I thought about the interaction with the Marine who worked at my recruiting station and thought, *Only God could have placed this opportunity in my lap, let's see where it goes!*

Embracing this opportunity, I underwent their extensive interview process, which included canvassing—knocking on 50 doors to gather names and numbers before being considered for employment. I told myself this was nothing compared to the dangers I had faced in Fallujah. After all, the risk of rejection was far preferable to being shot at or threatened by explosives.

Borah worked at a car dealership until Maddox was born, and I was still working but doing everything without pay. When I graduated in June, I was still undergoing the interview process with the financial services company, and they finally hired me, but it wasn't until September.

The following year, my faith was tested in several significant ways. Even though the circumstances were difficult, I stayed the course by relying on my faith and purpose. During my deployment, I applied what my financial advisor, Mike, taught me in Iraq: pay myself first. And I did, for a long time! Because of Mike's advice and expertise, I had savings in a brokerage account. I made impressive returns from Apple and other stocks, especially given that my only income was VA Disability, leaving my entire income for 2012 at just around

$13,000. After depleting every penny I had to take care of my family that year, I told Borah I was out of money.

Despite the hardships, we never missed a single mortgage payment, paying credit card bills, or anything. Borah and I continued attending church and being good people, but in my heart, I knew our ability to sustain ourselves was solely because of God and our faith in Him. God would remove any giant from our lives. We just had to believe.

By fall, the company I spent months interviewing for hired me as a financial advisor, and as timing would have it, I got an offer from the FBI that winter. I didn't think there would be a problem until I realized I loved investing. Borah and I prayed about it. The question was, "Where does God want me to be?" The Holy Spirit was like, *I am going to slap you real quick, so you pay attention*, and suddenly, I knew. I was a husband and a father first. The FBI drilled into me that 40% of the year I'd be away from home. Given the timing of everything, it created an internal conflict.

There's a difference between a career and a calling. You work toward a career and earn an income to support your family, but it doesn't fulfill who God designed you to be. A calling gives you a greater sense of accomplishment because you are impacting others. While I felt the FBI would be a career, managing a financial practice and guiding my clients to make prudent decisions was my calling. I knew poverty and I knew loss. And I knew learning how to invest in the future could help countless others.

When I left the church service, I told Borah I was calling the FBI to decline the opportunity; they weren't happy about it. They reminded me of how much time and money they spent flying me to interviews, completing polygraphs, and everything involved, but I told them I had a son. I had to do what was best for my family. By trusting the Holy Spirit, I absolutely made the best decision.

Ephesians 4:1-3 reminded me that "As a prisoner for the Lord, then, I urge you to live a life worthy of the calling you have received. Be completely humble and gentle; be patient, bearing one another in love. Make every effort to keep the unity of the Spirit through the bond of peace." My time of fighting was over. I needed God to lead me to a place of humility, patience, and love. I found that through God, Borah, and now my newborn son Maddox, I never wanted to jeopardize those relationships by leaving for the FBI.

Sometimes people look at your success as a measure of their success. I had no intentions of joining the financial company to be average. Average could have gotten me killed in Iraq. Instead, within four years, I built my business wearing a suit and tie every day. I locked myself into a war mindset and knocked on over 1,200 doors without Dew kicking them off the hinges. I grew a successful business by having conversations on doorsteps. Failure, rejection, and letting my family down were my fears. Failure was not an option!

I used the same tactic that helped me discover my why. I wrote down my FEARs on one side of an index card, being rejection, letting my family down, and failure. I flipped it over, and then wrote down my WHYs. My number one "why" was to give my children a life I could have never dreamed of, followed by giving Borah a life she deserved, and finally to move my mom out of the trailer she lived in. To break the generational curse of a life of poverty that my family has known for as long as we can remember. Each evening as I pulled into our driveway, I would take the card out of my suit pocket and ask myself, "Which one did I choose today?"

After completely trusting God, my career took off, and I was doing exceptionally well. I started my own business as planned and put everything into it. Everything! Like Borah said, "Without God in our marriage, it would have been toast a long time ago. Faith is a huge component. We are all imperfect. We all fall short," and she was right.

My personal liberation has taken 16 years to realize, following trauma experienced in Iraq, leading to anger, depression, PTSD, and anxiety. It took meeting Borah and beginning therapy for me to face my Goliath. Through Eye Movement Desensitization and Reprocessing (EMDR) Therapy, I have started processing these traumas, a process both overwhelming and freeing. This journey, inspired by conversations with Johnnie and Borah, made me confront the fact that I needed help.

With God as the foundation of our lives, Borah and I built something special. Maddox's birth changed my mindset and focus on family, which had grown to four boys. Ayden was Borah's first son, born in 2006, then following Maddox, Titus Jaymes came along in 2013 and Aurelius Jon rounded out the family as our the youngest in 2017. Our faith is the reason Borah and I are together. After what I'd been through, it's the only reason. I can't help but feel for people because some have severe mental problems. Some people don't tap into their adversities to become better. The problem is that instead, we carry it with us forever. Devoting myself to Christ is how I overcame mine—how Borah and I accomplished it together.

Johnnie and I, alongside Borah, Parris, my brothers, and countless others, have locked horns with Goliath—the menacing behemoth of mental health. We've navigated the labyrinthine contours of human emotions, understanding why some individuals wall themselves off, permitting the wounds to fester in silence, much like an unchecked terminal illness.

Our silence often emanates from fear, a paucity of trust, or perhaps the lack of resources and financial support to seek help. Over time, we've learned that breaking the silence, speaking out, and surrendering our anguish to a higher power for resolution offers a healthier path. We each had to find our motive, our raison d'être—why we persist, why we choose a particular career path, start a family, set goals, pursue happiness, live in a specific region, seek divorce, end friendships, or instigate change in our lives when grappling with mental health challenges.

My mission is to delve into people's stories—to explore how they confronted their Goliath and understand who they've become. I want to unearth the forces that shaped them, to know if they believed in their capacity to vanquish their Goliath, or why they felt they couldn't. From there, we continue the conversation. The war with my mental Goliath is ongoing, but progress is being made. Whatever you need to do to be healthy for yourself—please care enough to take those steps.

I learned that when God gives us a challenge, He wants us to fight to overcome it, even our toughest battles with the worst outlook, so we can see who He is and why we need Him. He wants us to see the strength he planted inside of us. It's up to us to water that mustard seed and nurture its growth. If I wanted to make a difference and allow God to use me, He made sure I heard him. I still have the strength to fight the next battle—because the battles keep coming, we just become more equipped with how to handle them.

# ULTRA(SOUND)

## FORGE • AHEAD

**AN ULTRASOUND CAN REVEAL** the beauty and complexities of the human body, even in the early stages of life. We use an ultrasound as a non-invasive way to see beyond the surface. It can detect the heartbeat of a newborn child such as Maddox, who brings joy and happiness, or it can reveal a hidden tumor or illness in the case of Rocky. Tools and technology are available for us to better understand what is happening within and around us. When I heard Maddox's heartbeat, it rattled my soul. I needed to become a better person for my son and for Borah.

Not only did the ultrasound reveal a healthy heart, but it also revealed that I had an opportunity to break the generational curse that my family had carried. By examining the inner workings of our bodies or a situation, we can gain valuable insights and informed decisions. Looking at your own life, what needs to be revealed that is hiding behind the surface? Maybe it's forgiveness that you carry or resentment for a situation that was always out of your control. The longer you hold those feelings, the longer you give your mental giant authority to grow and pull you into the deepest, darkest pit known to man.

It's time to remove whatever's causing the pain, suture the wounds, and nurture them so that they heal without leaving scars. If you are struggling to figure out how to examine your life in a positive way to better your mental health, here are five ways to create a positive mental health outcome, your own "ultrasound:"

- **JOURNALING**: Reflect on your thoughts, emotions, and experiences through maintaining a journal. This strategy can help you gain insights into patterns, triggers, and positive aspects of your life.

- **MEDITATION**: Utilize different apps that offer guided mindfulness or meditation sessions. These tools can help you stay present, manage stress, and promote a positive mental state.

- **SELF-ASSESSMENT QUESTIONNAIRE**: Find a reputable mental health website that provides a mental health assessment questionnaire that can help you identify areas of concern and access your overall well-being.

- **THERAPEUTIC WORKSHEETS**: *There are various worksheets and workbooks online to help you explore and address specific aspects of your life, such as gratitude, goal setting, or self-reflection.*

- **LIFE AUDIT EXERCISE**: *Evaluate different life domains and assess your satisfaction and fulfillment in each such as relationships, work, hobbies, etc. Identify areas of improvement and set realistic goals for positive change.*

*The hardest step with any change is the first stride. Take one stride today in the right direction for overcoming your mental health Goliath!*

*Borah, thank you.*

# JOHNN(Y)

# go(liath)

## JOHNN(Y)IE

**WHEN WE LOOK AT** one another, we know what the world sees: one white Johnny, one black Johnnie. When you hear us talk, one is from the country, one is from the hood. Black, White, Hispanic, Asian, American Indian, whatever we are, the world is teaching us that if we're different, we're not supposed to have anything in common. But that's a lie.

In the high-stakes world of collegiate athletics, just as in the crucible of military service, there's an undercurrent of a daunting reality. It's the narrative of hope, often sold as a surefire path to glory. But beneath the veneer of promised success lies a stark truth: there's no guarantee, no "Plan B" etched out for these individuals. When the uniform comes off—be it a jersey or fatigues—the identity that's been forged and worn like armor is suddenly stripped away, leaving a void that echoes with the question, "What now?"

For many, the landing is rough, the transition jarring. The ground that once felt solid underfoot as a football player or the certainty that came with being part of a unit in the service now seems to give way. It's where some, teetering on the edge of mental instability, face the darkest of battles within.

Finding peace often means turning to faith, looking through the lens of compassion and empathy rather than division. It's a profound journey, from seeing others as the "enemy" to brothers and sisters in humanity. It's a path that leads from isolation to community, from resentment to understanding.

Drawing strength from our disparate backgrounds and distinct life trajectories, we were two boys— ironically both named Johnny/ie—out of countless children, tempered by the furnace of adversity. Yet, as our paths converged, we discovered significant shared ground in our individual journeys, families, values, growth, and spiritual convictions.

Everybody has something in common. Shared experiences, emotions, and desires all connect us through our collective human existence. We wouldn't have known we had so many similarities if we didn't make the effort to spend time together. The best way to learn more about a person is to do activities together. Do the weird stuff that reveals more of their authentic self and yours! Indulge in the uncomfortable rather than the comfortable so you can pull back that mask that nearly everyone in society wears at one time or another.

We're facing a mental health crisis. Suicide rates are higher than they've ever been. Men, women, children, and the majority of society have shown that we have the propensity to mask who we are, our feelings, truths, and a plethora of issues. We don't express ourselves adequately, if at all. We have a moral imperative to prioritize mental health and vanquish this formidable giant.

As men, for some of us, our mindset has been shaped to think we can do anything and withstand anything. Showing weakness and crying or admitting when we are hurting was not always widely accepted. It wasn't normal. It still isn't considered normal.

Somehow, we need to get to a point where we can realize and accept when we need help, even if that reality comes from someone who cares about us. Maybe they have noticed that our behaviors have changed or that we're in a different or darker place. It might be as simple as finding a therapist or mentor to help you adjust to a change in career, loss of loved ones, or life in general. Many don't seek the professional help that is needed—and for some, it's because they can't afford it.

For a decade, we stood shoulder to shoulder with individuals who embodied the heart of this nation, witnessing firsthand the strife, fear, and adversity etched on their faces. As a nation, we are caught in a conflict within ourselves, playing into the desires of our adversaries. Yet, our most profound shortcoming is rooted in our failure to engage one another in dialogue that is elevating, therapeutic, wholesome, truthful, and imbued with compassion. We created such dialogue between each other to foster empathy without judgment and provide space for sharing our truths and pains. The goal is to participate in building a resilient society, one ready to stand united against our shared adversities, our metaphorical Goliaths.

We want you to initiate these discussions to encourage faith, bolster mental and physical health, and foster unity. Through our struggles, we can emerge stronger, acting as God's warriors for others. We must focus on overcoming our daily challenges rather than dwelling on them. Identifying and tackling your Goliath demands vulnerability and honest communication. It could be generational poverty, substance abuse, painful experiences, or mental health—Goliath can be vanquished. The fight might be challenging, but victory promises a better future for generations to come.

We must believe that God is bigger than all of our problems—because He is.

Fear is a potent weapon wielded by your Goliath. It is a barrier between your dreams and aspirations, building a happy and healthy future, and making necessary life changes. Conversely, overcoming fear allows you to follow your divine purpose and path.

Drawing inspiration from David versus Goliath, there are three primary tactics used by Goliath: engendering fear, seeking destruction, and enforcing imprisonment. Goliath magnifies fear, distorting reality. Counteracting this requires listing your fears against your reasons to overcome them, focusing on solutions rather than problems.

The second tactic, destruction, targets your dreams, happiness, and purpose. Your Goliath aims to hold you captive, just as Goliath intended to do to the children of Israel. Combating this requires assembling an army of support: therapists, family, friends, and faith communities.

The final tactic is generational imprisonment, such as addiction, poverty, or mental health—Goliath aims to trap you in the same cycle. Recognizing and understanding this type of imprisonment is the first step toward liberation and healing.

You possess the capacity to overcome the formidable Goliath of mental challenges looming within your psyche. This victory lies within your grasp as you discern the tactics it employs, navigate the labyrinth of fear, and tenaciously adhere to your reasons for triumph. Embrace the unwavering conviction that you, too, possess the ability to topple your personal Goliath!

We all have the same commodity of time—24 hours a day to make decisions, form attitudes, and keep commitments. The true meaning of success is the ability to create time. Time to decide and be with the ones you love. Time to create space when you need to look inward, with the ability to reflect on your own mental health without the outside pressures of a job and commitments. Conquering your Goliath can be like the components of a clock. Every clock or watch typically has five components:

1. The weight or spring provides energy to help turn the hands of the clock.

2. The weight gear train assists with rewinding the weight drum, so you don't need to rewind the clock every day.

3. The escapement is made of a pendulum that regulates the speed at which the energy of the weight is released.

4. The hand gear train regulates the minute and hour hands, so they turn at the correct rates of speed.

5. The setting mechanism is the tiny wheel that disengages and slips or ratchets the gear train so the clock can be rewound and set.

In the face of adversity, we often discover similar components within ourselves, aiding us in creating time and comprehending our mental health struggles. To overcome our metaphorical yet generational Goliaths, consider these elements of your mental health clock:

- **MINDSET:** Realize you are worthy of more by focusing your energy on your own mindset. You are not put on this planet to struggle; you have a purpose and are worthy of any dream you may have. Therefore, you must create the mindset of believing you are worthy of your purpose.

- **FAITH:** Giving your troubles to God while discovering the core principles from which we have been created can lead you to a place of peace if you are vulnerable enough to allow the word of God to guide you.

- **COMMUNITY:** Realizing you cannot isolate your thoughts and allow them to consume your energy. Isolation can destroy time and your mindset. Instead, reach out to your spouse, family, therapist, or mentors when needed. Create a community of those you trust around you and be vulnerable concerning your struggles. Some of the hardest discussions we've ever had were in writing this book, but they allowed us to heal and bond closer to our family.

- **PATIENCE**: Change is hard. Creating time and a healthy mindset is even more challenging. Today, we want immediate results. However, defeating your Goliath requires patience to allow yourself the ability to work toward creating the components needed to conquer your Goliath.

- **RESILIENCE**: The ability to recover quickly from difficulties or to spring back into shape. Just as a clock needs to spring back to the correct time, we must embody resilience through every adversity. If you cannot create resilience through the adversities, you have and will face, that can result in isolation, among other detriments.

For those who've served, who've played the game at its highest level, awareness is everything. Awareness is recognizing when the darkness begins to creep back in, when the old ways of thinking threaten to resurface. There's no magic cure, no final whistle in the game against mental challenges. Instead, it's a daily commitment to seek help, to find solace in prayer, in family, in camaraderie.

Isolation is the enemy of healing. It's a spiral that tightens its grip, pulling down to depths that can seem inescapable. Yet, the antidote lies in connection—in the courage to be vulnerable, to share struggles, and to embrace the collective strength of shared burdens.

Isolation can serve as a catalyst for mental health issues, often precipitating conditions like depression. This condition can be exacerbated by a lack of social interaction, where feelings of loneliness and disconnectedness can lead to significant distress. This is why it's crucial to maintain connections and seek help when feeling isolated or detached. It's always important to remember that assistance is available, and reaching out can be a decisive step toward healing and recovery.

The deep sense of isolation that some individuals experience can contribute to their decision to take their own lives. It's a heart-wrenching reality and a persistent issue in many communities, including among veterans and active-duty military personnel like the Marines. These individuals may struggle with the aftermath of traumatic experiences or the challenges of readjusting to civilian life, leading to feelings of alienation and loneliness.

This underlines the importance of strong support networks and regular, open communication. People must maintain contact with their loved ones, particularly those struggling with mental health issues. Reaching out to them, showing empathy, and encouraging them to seek help can make a significant difference. Also, accessible mental health services can provide professional support and treatment for individuals in need.

Prevention of suicide requires a comprehensive approach that encompasses all sectors of society and includes both support from loved ones and professional help. By building these networks of support, we can hope to reach those who are feeling isolated and help them navigate their way through their struggles.

In both arenas, the lesson is clear: the battle for mental wellness is ongoing. It's a road marked by continuous effort, where healing is not a destination but a journey. It's about growing each day as a spouse, a parent, a friend, a leader—finding purpose in the lessons of the past to forge a future where every moment is a step toward victory over one's personal Goliaths.

We both grappled with isolation at different levels, which gave rise to some of the worst thoughts, feelings, and depression we have ever experienced. If you find yourself in this situation, we are begging you at this moment to put down this book, call a friend or someone you trust, and just cry. Release your worries onto that person and seek the components listed above to create time, your own mental health freedom, and conquer your Goliath.

You are not alone.

*To you, thank you.*

## FORGE AHEAD

Love,

Johnn(y)ie

You are not alone!

Call 988 and you will find that
your life has tremendous value.

# ENCOURAGING VERSES

Psalm 34:17-18 - "The righteous cry out, and the LORD hears them; he delivers them from all their troubles. The LORD is close to the brokenhearted and saves those who are crushed in spirit."

Psalm 147:3 - "He heals the brokenhearted and binds up their wounds."

Isaiah 41:10 - "So do not fear, for I am with you; do not be dismayed, for I am your God. I will strengthen you and help you; I will uphold you with my righteous right hand."

Matthew 11:28-29 - "Come to me, all you who are weary and burdened, and I will give you rest. Take my yoke upon you and learn from me, for I am gentle and humble in heart, and you will find rest for your souls."

2 Corinthians 1:3-4 - "Praise be to the God and Father of our Lord Jesus Christ, the Father of compassion and the God of all comfort, who comforts us in all our troubles, so that we can comfort those in any trouble with the comfort we ourselves receive from God."

Philippians 4:6-7 - "Do not be anxious about anything, but in every situation, by prayer and petition, with thanksgiving, present your requests to God. And the peace of God, which transcends all understanding, will guard your hearts and your minds in Christ Jesus."

1 Peter 5:7 - "Cast all your anxiety on him because he cares for you."

Psalm 40:1-2 - "I waited patiently for the LORD; he turned to me and heard my cry. He lifted me out of the slimy pit, out of the mud and mire; he set my feet on a rock and gave me a firm place to stand."

Psalm 42:11 - "Why, my soul, are you downcast? Why so disturbed within me? Put your hope in God, for I will yet praise him, my Savior and my God."

Romans 8:38-39 - "For I am convinced that neither death nor life, neither angels nor demons, neither the present nor the future, nor any powers, neither height nor depth, nor anything else in all creation, will be able to separate us from the love of God that is in Christ Jesus our Lord."

# RESOURCES

## GENERAL MENTAL HEALTH RESOURCES

### National Alliance on Mental Illness (NAMI)
- Website: nami.org
- Offers support, education, and advocacy for individuals and families affected by mental illness.

### Mental Health America (MHA)
- Website: mhanational.org
- Provides extensive resources on mental health, including tools for finding mental health care and support.

## PTSD-SPECIFIC RESOURCES

### National Center for PTSD
- Website: ptsd.va.gov
- Offers resources and information specifically focused on PTSD, including self-help tools and information on treatment options.

### PTSD Alliance
- Website: ptsdalliance.org
- A group of organizations dedicated to increasing awareness about PTSD.

# DEPRESSION-SPECIFIC RESOURCES

### Depression and Bipolar Support Alliance (DBSA)
- Website: dbsalliance.org
- Provides information on depression and bipolar disorder, online support groups, and tools for finding in-person support.

### American Foundation for Suicide Prevention
- Website: afsp.org
- Focuses on reducing the loss of life from suicide through research, education, and advocacy.

# SUICIDE PREVENTION RESOURCES

### National Suicide Prevention Lifeline
- Phone: 1-800-273-TALK (1-800-273-8255)
- Website: suicidepreventionlifeline.org
- A 24-hour, toll-free, confidential suicide prevention hotline available to anyone in suicidal crisis or emotional distress.

### Crisis Text Line
- Text HOME to 741741 in the US
- Website: crisistextline.org
- Offers 24/7 support via text from trained crisis counselors.

## INTERNATIONAL RESOURCES

### Befrienders Worldwide
- Website: befrienders.org
- Provides information on suicide and emotional support services worldwide.

### International Association for Suicide Prevention (IASP)
- Website: iasp.info
- Offers resources and support for suicide prevention globally.


## SELF-HELP AND EDUCATION

### MoodGYM
- Website: moodgym.com.au
- An interactive self-help program for depression and anxiety.

### Psychology Today Therapist Finder
- Website: psychologytoday.com/us/therapists
- A tool for finding therapists and mental health professionals in your area.

For PTSD:

- "The Body Keeps the Score: Brain, Mind, and Body in the Healing of Trauma" by Bessel van der Kolk
  Explores the impact of trauma on the body and mind and discusses various paths for recovery.
- "Waking the Tiger: Healing Trauma" by Peter A. Levine
  Introduces the concept of somatic experiencing, a therapeutic approach to healing trauma.

For Depression:

- "Feeling Good: The New Mood Therapy" by David D. Burns
  A guide to cognitive behavioral therapy (CBT) techniques for overcoming depression.
- "The Mindful Way through Depression: Freeing Yourself from Chronic Unhappiness" by Mark Williams, John Teasdale, Zindel Segal, and Jon Kabat-Zinn
  Combines mindfulness practices with cognitive therapy to address the root causes of depression.

**For Suicidal Thoughts:**

- **"Night Falls Fast: Understanding Suicide"** by Kay Redfield Jamison
  Explores the psychological aspects of suicide, combined with personal narratives.
- **"Reasons to Stay Alive"** by Matt Haig
  A memoir that discusses the author's struggle with depression and suicidal thoughts, offering hope and reassurance.

## MOBILE APPS

**For PTSD:**

- **PTSD Coach**
  Developed by the U.S. Department of Veterans Affairs, this app provides users with tools and resources to manage stress and PTSD symptoms.
- **CPT Coach**
  Also by the U.S. Department of Veterans Affairs, designed to support Cognitive Processing Therapy, a specific type of PTSD treatment.

**For Depression:**

- **Moodfit**
  A mental health app that provides tools to

help understand and improve your mood, including mood tracking and cognitive behavioral therapy exercises.

- **Headspace**
  An app offering guided meditations, many of which can be helpful for managing depression and anxiety.

**For Suicidal Thoughts and Crisis Management:**

- **MY3**
  Designed for people who are struggling with suicidal thoughts, it helps create a support network and safety plan.
- **Stay Alive**
  Offers help and support for people having thoughts of suicide and those worried about someone else.

# ACKNOWLEDGMENTS

Sharing a story of vulnerability takes a tremendous amount of courage. This book has been in the making for nearly two years and we have battled the exposure our stories bring to a world full of judgment. Writing a memoir is not just a solitary endeavor; it is a collective effort supported by love, encouragement, and sacrifices of many who are involved. Writing our stories has been one of the most challenging, but rewarding journeys we have faced that could not have been done with the support of our families and wives. We are deeply grateful to those who have played a pivotal role in shaping our story.

*To our mothers*, your unwavering support, boundless love, and profound courage to preserve through a life of struggle has been the guiding light through the darkest times. Your strength and resilience have inspired us to preserve and strive for greatness. We both cannot thank you, Julie and Latoya, enough for facing the many mountains and valleys while always placing your children first.

*To our fathers*, we don't hold resentment in our hearts or blame you for anything that occurred in our childhood. Instead, we thank you. If it weren't for the adversities we faced and the maturity we needed to develop at a young age, we would have become completely different people. We will never wish our journey to change but want you to know we love you and appreciate the lessons you gave us throughout our life.

*Keith*, I can't thank you enough for the traits, such as work ethic and accountability, that you taught me throughout my life. I know being a stepfather is one of the hardest positions to be in and I commend you for raising Jesse and me as your own. We didn't have a lot, but you ensured that we had everything we needed growing up and I will be forever grateful.

*To my siblings*, first off, I love y'all so much! You guys don't know how much you all have pushed me through the ups and the downs. I want to thank y'all for always supporting me on this journey. Through it all, y'all have always been on my mind. I know life hasn't been perfect for us, but I really hope that I made all of you proud and been the big brother that y'all needed. Love, Johnnie

*Jesse*, I understand a lot changed during my time in war. I'm so sorry I wasn't always there for you in the years you needed it most, becoming a teenager and a young adult. I love you very much and will always support you in anything you seek to do and I'm so thankful to have you as a brother.

*To Borah and Viv*, your unwavering love, patience, and understanding have been the pillars of strength that have sustained us through the highs and lows of this journey. Your belief in both of us has been the fuel we each needed when the path seemed daunting, and life felt hopeless. When our mental struggles were at our peak you never seemed to judge or waver from the love and support you provided. Without your encouragement, not only would this story not exist to help others, but we could very well be stuck in the pit of misery you found us in.

*To our children*, you changed the course of our entire life. You are the joy and inspiration behind everything we do. Your laughter, curiosity, and boundless energy remind us of the beauty and resilience of the human spirit. Thank you for your patience, understanding, and endless love as we have poured ourselves into this project. You are our greatest motivation, and we are endlessly grateful to be your father.

*To Veterans and athletes*, we are also deeply grateful to you who have entrusted us to be a part of their journeys with those who inspired us to be better along the way.

*To Marines* Matt Black, Ruben, Hackler, Harder, Doc Sep, Sgt Brodin, Clevenger, Fortune, Dew, Mike Connole, 2nd Battalion 7th Marines, Echo Company, 1st Platoon. Regimental Combat Team 7, - JUMP - Ripper Red, the love I have for you and the honor to serve a long side of you in the hellish places on earth will be my highest honor. Thank you for your inspiration and dedication to this Nation, I will always be grateful. Semper Fidelis, Johnny

*To the Collins Family*, every day I see Jon's face. I will never forget his infectious laughter and love for life. It pains me each day that I was not able to serve alongside him and Davidson in Iraq and I will never forget the sacrifice he and your family has made for this Nation and my children. I will forever be in his debt. Love, Johnny

**To the Buckeyes and Dwyer High School**, Parris, Kwon, Kato, The Pak, Coach Myer, Stewie, Coach Daniels, and many more, one of my greatest achievements was playing alongside and being coached by you. The lessons I learned will always be carried on throughout my life and passed down to my children. Thank you for always encouraging me to be better while never giving up on me as a player and friend. Love, Johnnie

**To our mentors, friends, and colleagues** who have offered us guidance, support, and invaluable insights along the way, thank you for your unwavering belief in us. You pushed us to new heights of self-discovery and growth. Marla, thank you for your willingness to take on this project, offering not only your writing ability and profound intuition, but most importantly, encouragement and support. Thank you for talking us through some of the darkest times in our life without judgment. Lauren and your team, we cannot thank you enough for the assistance with design, illustration, and structure. Your patience and guidance through this journey have been invaluable and we are forever grateful. Thank you.

**Faith mentors**, through the beginning of my faith journey, I am forever grateful for the conversations and lessons you taught me as I transitioned from the Marines, to becoming a father and husband led by my faith. Dave Staten, Ely Conrad, Pastor Ken, and Pastor Dale—thank you for mentoring me as a young adult while leading me to develop a relationship with Christ and becoming a better man while showing empathy for others. I am so thankful. Johnny

**Finally, to you the reader**, thank you for your openness, your empathy, and your willingness to engage with the stories shared within these pages. It is our sincerest hope that this memoir sparks conversations, fosters understanding, and offers hope to those who may be struggling with their own mental Goliaths.

Always remember, **FORGE AHEAD**.

With deepest appreciation,

johnn(y)ie

# ABOUT THE AUTHORS

**JOHNNY DAWSON** was born in Columbus, Ohio and spent his childhood in Butcher Hollow, Kentucky. He graduated from Circleville High School and found himself in Iraq just eight months later. A Marine Combat Veteran with multiple combat deployments to Iraq in support of Operation Iraqi Freedom along with serving in the first Battle of Fallujah in 2004, Johnny then provided personal security for 7th Marines Regimental Colonel Crowe in the Al Anbar Province.

In addition to his service, he assisted with protection details as an intern with the Secret Service for President Obama, Vice President Biden, Governor Romney, and House Speaker Paul Ryan in 2012. That same year, Johnny became the first person in his family to obtain a college degree, graduating from The Ohio State University.

After declining his dream job with the FBI following the birth of his son Maddox, he pursued a career in finance, becoming a successful CEO and Private Wealth Advisor. Today, he manages nearly $350 million in assets under management for his clients. Johnny has been featured in the magazine *On Wall Street*, awarded the Columbus Business First 40 under 40, along with Forbes best-in-state Wealth Management Teams for Ohio.

Today, Johnny and Borah have four sons: Ayden, Maddox, Titus, and Aurelius. In addition to his work in finance, he coaches his son's youth athletic teams in hockey, baseball, and football. Johnny has led the Hilliard Colts baseball team from 2021 to 2023 with a record of 82-21, with multiple championships including Ohio State Champions in 2023. He instills values of a positive mindset and upstanding character in the youth he coaches, hopeful they can carry lessons from the ball diamond, field, or ice rink to life as adults.

Johnny is dedicated to giving back to his community through leadership and fostering discussions around mental health for Veterans. He often speaks at conferences and business leadership meetings about overcoming your fear by finding your why using his experiences in combat and entrepreneurship.

Johnny created a 12-week long Bible Study that focuses on the effects of PTSD and how we can use our faith to find peace when dealing with PTSD. His hope is to continue nurturing tough conversations that will provide healing to Veterans and men who struggle with the mental Goliaths they may encounter in life.

**JOHNNIE DIXON, III** was born in West Palm Beach, Florida where he graduated from Dwyer High School as a four-star recruit. He first found success in football when he helped Dwyer win its second Florida Class 7A State Championship and their first-ever perfect season (15-0). Johnnie was named second team all-state in 2013 and played his best football game in the state playoffs with 17 receptions for 366 yards and six touchdowns in Dwyer's five-game run to the state title. Rated the 34th prospect in the nation on the ESPN 300 and its' fifth rated wide receiver, Johnnie committed to The Ohio State University in 2014.

Johnnie battled through injuries in 2014, but still assisted the Buckeyes in their win at the first College Football Playoff National Championship. In 2015, Johnnie's ongoing recovery from injuries led to depression and mental health struggles. However, Johnnie made a comeback in 2017 and 2018 to achieve a combined 1,111 reception yards and 16 touchdowns with the Buckeyes.

Johnnie is the first person in his family to graduate from a college university with a degree in Sociology and Human Development and Family Services. Johnnie signed with the Houston Texans as an undrafted free agent following the 2019 NFL draft, then moved to the Arizona Cardinals practice squad.

Johnnie was eventually placed on injured reserve and was then signed with the Dallas Cowboys where he caught his first NFL touchdown pass during a pre-season game in 2021. Again, however, he was released following roster cuts.

Johnnie found success in the USFL with the New Orleans Breakers as a starting receiver, leading the team in both receptions and touchdowns registering 37 receptions for 359 yards and four touchdowns. Johnnie today lives in Arizona with his wife Viv, their son Johnnie Dixon, IV, and daughter Zya.

Today, Johnnie has a passion for being in the kitchen and cooking for his family and friends. He also enjoys photography and aspires to become an actor one day. Johnnie is focused on helping athletes overcome their anxiety and depression stemming from sports-related injuries. Using his first-hand knowledge of the metaphorical Goliaths athletes face today, Johnnie also wants to help athletes prepare for and adjust to life after football.

Printed in the USA
CPSIA information can be obtained
at www.ICGtesting.com
JSHW011337031124
72875JS00004B/11

9 781950 476947